CONFUSION, COMPASSION, CONFESSION

CONFUSION, COMPASSION, CONFESSION

A Married Woman's Dilemma

ATHRA BODHI'S

Enlightened Publishing 4 You

Confusion, Compassion, Confession: A Married Woman's Dilemma
Copyright © 2024 Athra Bodhi All rights reserved
Published by
Enlightened Publishing 4 You, LLC

No part of this book may be used or reproduced by any means, graphic, electronic, or mechanical, including production with artificial intelligence, photocopying, recording, taping, or by any information storage retrieval system without the written permission of the author except in cases of brief quotations embodied in critical articles and reviews.
Purchase only authorized editions of this book.
Due to the dynamic nature of the Internet, any web addresses and links listed in Important Information may be invalid since the publication of this book.
The author of this book does not attempt to dispense mental counseling or medical advice in any form. Individuals are explicitly encouraged to seek mental counseling and medical advice, including substance abuse, from a licensed professional to diagnose and treat any type of symptoms being experienced. The intent of the author is to provide enlightenment and spiritual encouragement.
Identifiers: Library of Congress Control Number: 2024900592
ISBN 9780999117767(Hardcover) /9780999117781 (Paperback)/ 9780999117774 (ebook)

First Edition: February 2024

This book is dedicated to
Regenia, James, Ethel, and Donald
who believed in tolerance and acceptance.

Contents

Dedication v

THE PAINTED PICTURE

1 In The Middle of the Night 2

ADRIANA'S WEDDING DAY

2 In the Beginning 6
3 Cilicia 21

STILL HAVING AND STILL HOLDING

4 Dear Diary 26
5 Seventeen Years Later 29
6 September, Awareness Month 32
7 Pushing Boundaries 43
8 Borderlines 52
9 I Know I Love My Husband 60
10 He Loves His Wife 68

LADY LAZARUS

11	Feeling Vulnerable	74
12	Fight For Your Husband, Chile	83
13	The Kiss of Death	89

IN THE EYE OF THE HURRICANE

14	The Eye of the Storm	112
15	My Love is Too Delicaate	120
16	Comfort in the Storm	133

SPIRITUAL GUIDANCE

FOR WOMEN WHO HAVE ATTEMPTED SUICIDE: THE RAINBOW IS MORE THAN ENOUGH

17	The 85-15 Support Group	143
18	Leviticus	150
19	Confession	163
20	The Hummingbird	175
21	Matthew 19:12	183
22	If You Let Me Stay	193

MAKING THE RAINBOW ENOUGH

23	Compassion	212
24	Letting Go of Pain	222

25	Because This World Is Mine	233
26	From This Day Forward	245

Important Information — 259
The Chakra System — 261
Notes — 263
Book Club Questions — 267
Resources — 269
About The Author — 271

The Painted Picture

It's all a painted picture;
Imagery as done by a poet;
Dreaming has become to me
Some sort of fancy sport.

Life can be so nice,
Or at least that is what they say;
But every time I get a grip on it,
It does all but stay that way.

A painted picture is nice,
Like when a person gets flatter;
But when the picture is no longer painted perfect,
It is just like glass; it will shatter!

I

In The Middle of the Night

Lying in her bed, Adriana rolled from her right side to her stomach. She slid a little closer to the right side of the bed. Finally, she could reach his pillow. She tucked the pillow under her body just to feel close to him. She closed her eyes and inhaled; the pillow had his scent on it.

Her annual "Before School Spa Day" with Cilicia was much different this year. They talked about their upcoming school year – changes in educational standards and psychological evaluations; anxieties about the teacher and school psychologist shortages; changes in district and school leadership and what those changes might mean; and balancing their careers with parenting and being wives. All of that was a part of their usual conversations.

It was the picture Cilicia had shown her that turned the conversation to left field. It was the suspicions Cilicia shared that had her mind doing cartwheels and disrupting her sleep.

Adriana always knew that Cilicia and Justus had marital problems; she had shared as much on several occasions. The allusion that

Gavin was somehow involved with Justus's excursions was the thing that made today's conversation different.

She held her breath. "One.. Two.. Three.." she counted in her head. She exhaled. Another breath. "One... Two.. Three... Four..." Again, an exhale. The lump in her throat would not allow her to swallow. It would not allow her to cry. She blinked two times, three times, four times.

She closed her eyes. She held her breath. She pulled his other pillow into her arms then put her face into it. She could smell him.

The darkness of the room didn't help how she was feeling. The delta waves sleep video was of very little help. She could not get it out of her mind. The darkness was consuming her; she could not move.

"Are you there, God?" she whispered.

Silence.

She embraced the pillow a little more.

"Are you there?" she whispered. "Please, answer me."

She rolled from her stomach to her back. Finally, the tears came.

"I have done everything required of me. I don't ask for much. When you speak, I listen. I need YOU to speak to me now."

Silence.

She closed her eyes and tried to clear the lump in her throat. She waited; no answer.

She stared at the ceiling. She swallowed. She exhaled.

No answer.

She inhaled, then rolled back to her stomach. She reached for the pillow she had kicked to the floor that belonged to him.

She inched her body over it. She tucked it below her waist then wrapped her legs around it again. She pushed it in just a little more.

He wasn't there, but she wanted to feel him. Being close to him was the security that gave her the strength to face each day.

Tonight was different. He wasn't there.

She closed her eyes and allowed the tears to carry her to a place that might bring her back to where she needed to be.

Adriana's Wedding Day

To Have and To Hold

2

In the Beginning

Adriana looked out her hotel window. It was the second day of Spring, so she thanked God for a crisp, March afternoon. The twenty-one days forecast had predicted a forty-percent chance of rain; however, the chances of rain had decreased over the past eight days. Adriana was saying one last prayer hoping that Tempestas had better things to attend to than to send a sudden storm to the south. She looked at the blue sky and noticed the slow-moving cirrus clouds. She exhaled with a smile, "You've answered my prayers."

Before she could get any deeper into her meditation, there was a knock at the door followed by the sound that told her it had been unlocked.

Adriana looked over her shoulder. She began to turn away from the window to face the person who was interrupting her peace.

Gliding from the door to the window in her silk, rose-gold matron of honor dress was Cilicia, her best friend from college. The off-shoulder bodice gave notice to her flawless, caramel, brown shoulders that had been sculpted, as if she was a goddess, from her years to being a cheerleader. She was tall and very beautiful with shoulders, length, wavy, black hair.

"We are leaving now," she said, the cue that alerted Adriana to the fact that her life was only moments away from forever changing.

Cilicia joined Adriana at the window that stretched from ceiling to floor. She gave her friend a hug then asked, "Are you ready?"

Trying her best not to cry, Adriana answered with starry eyes, "I'm ready."

"Then, we'll see you there," was accompanied by a gradual release of the bride's hands.

"See you there," with a slight hug then her return to gazing out the window.

Charlotte, North Carolina was Adriana's favorite place to be; it was her home away from home. Being on the fifteenth floor gave her a view of the city that allowed her to reminisce about the exciting times she had with her cousins and friends. She could look up Tryon Street and remember one of their favorite nighttime establishments from her early twenties.

Fat Tuesdays was where she and her cousins celebrated turning legal. They would sit at the bar and sample every daiquiri flavor from every machine. Those days ended when their favorite emancipation spot was replaced by Discovery Place.

"So long daiquiri bar; hello science center," she uttered to herself.

Adriana looked towards South Boulevard. Buildings were blocking the view of the thoroughfare she used to take with her cousins and friends. They spent many late nights during winter and spring breaks in their first year of college trying to exert the independence they enjoyed away from home. "Yep, we were Plum Crazy in those days."

She thought about the trips she had taken with her other roommate after her freshman year. First it was the Memorial Day weekend in Myrtle Beach for Bike Week. Then came the cruise to celebrate her stepsister's graduation from pharmacy school. It was on that cruise she had met the man she thought would become her husband.

She shook her head, "No." She quickly changed her thoughts to the man who was waiting for her to join him less than a mile away. The man who had recognized she was in some sort of pain. The man who had promised to love her past the pain of her last love.

"God, I thank you for allowing me to have the patience to trust you. I thank you for giving me the strength to believe in all the promises you made to me when I had lost my faith."

Adriana looked onto the street. She saw her father approaching the building. She knew it was time for her to go. She surveyed the Presidential Suite that had been her home for the past two nights. It was a bridal shower gift from her grandmother to her oldest princess.

"I want you and the girls to have a lovely time," Grandma Ethel told her. "You deserve it."

Adriana and Grandma Ethel shared a close relationship. She could talk to her grandmother about things she could not talk about with her mother. Grandma Ethel was truly her first best friend.

The familiar door sound prompted Adriana to bring her thoughts to the present moment.

"Okay, young lady," Marvin said to his only daughter.

"Okay, Daddy," Adriana said with a slight smile.

"Grandma Ethel sent you this fur for the ride to the museum," Marvin said, holding the Mahogany, mink cape to drape around Adriana's shoulders.

Adriana stood and watched her father's reflection in the window as he placed the fur around her shoulders.

"Are you ready to give me another son?" he asked.

"If that's what you want to call him, Old Man," was the jovial response Adriana gave her father.

"Old man? Who's an old man?" came the usual reply with a smile.

"Is this something old or borrowed?" Adrian inquired.

"I know it is something old. As far as being borrowed, your grandmother would be the one to answer that question."

"Since I don't really have anything borrowed, I will pretend that it is borrowed," Adriana rationalized to herself.

She slid her perfectly manicured hand into the right pocket of her skirt. The pocket was intentionally hidden by one of the boxed pleats. The softness of the silk was distinguished from the embroidered linen she had placed there for safe keeping.

She softly withdrew the treasure that was much older than she was. The treasure was indubitably a family heirloom. She gently displayed to her father the white linen that had yellowed a little over time. This fading was a testament to its longevity.

The perfectly squared linen was edged with lace that was woven with a rose on each corner. The interwoven lace edges had rose petals, leaves, and vines.

"Grandma Gina gave me this handkerchief that was given to her as a wedding gift from her grandmother. This is my something old," Adriana informed her father.

"Get out of here!" Marvin said in amazement. "That thing must be ninety years old."

"She said her grandma made it for her, so she was saving it for her granddaughter."

Marvin placed his left hand over his daughter's right hand. "I guess you had better put it back in your pocket. If you preserve it, you might be able to give it to my granddaughter on her wedding day."

"I will do my best," Adriana responded.

"Let me look at you one last time," Marvin requested. "My baby girl."

Adriana's small frame began to slowly turn on the ball of her left foot as if she were a mannequin on display. Resting on her pecan-colored skin was a plain, off white, silk bodice that capped her shoulders. Between the bodice and box pleats were marquise and solitaire shaped crystal rhinestones accented with pearls.

"Okay, Adriana La'Rosa. I hope you are ready."

"I've been ready since I woke up this morning."

"If you are not 100% sure, we can stay right here," Marvin said.

"Why would I not be 100% sure?" Adriana asked. "Gavin is a great guy, Dad. You said it yourself."

"Then Gavin it is," Marvin said as he extended his right elbow for his daughter to link with him.

Adriana looked at her dad and smiled with a knowingness that Gavin was most certainly the right man for her to spend the rest of her life with.

Marvin escorted his daughter out of the bridesmaid suite that would later become the honeymoon suite. He secretly knew that Adriana was his mother's favorite grandchild. She was more than happy to provide this suite for the young lady who bore part of her name – Ana.

Marvin and Regenia had done their best to uphold family traditions with names while honoring the uniqueness of their children. Anna Ethel was Adriana's paternal grandmother's name, and Regenia Rose was her maternal grandmother's name. Hence, Adriana La'Rosa Regenia was the name he and Regenia, the mother, had selected for their daughter almost twenty-five years ago.

Standing at five feet three inches, Adriana was the perfect blend of both sides of her family. Marvin treasured his mother's high cheekbones that complemented the almond shaped light, brown eyes that belonged to Grandma Gina. The long eyelashes were definitely a contribution from both grandmothers. Regenia, the mother, had always said that Adriana's nose was a mix between her mother's thin bridge and his mother's slight flare.

Marvin pulled his daughter close to him as he escorted her to the elevator. He wanted to hold on to her, to protect her just a little longer. Though, deep down inside, he knew that she would be well taken care of by the young man he had intimated but refused to be scared away three years ago.

Adriana glanced at her father with the thing he most cherished in his wife and his mother-in-law, their eyes. It was their eyes that told the truth about what they were thinking and feeling. It was those eyes that told him his baby girl trusted him and the man who would change her last name. Those eyes that made him say, "Yes" when he wanted to say, "No."

"You are looking at me almost like your mother did thirty-seven years ago," he said.

Marvin held his daughter's train as she stepped onto the elevator. He made sure she was secure in the car before pressing the "L" button.

"I never understood why women had to have such a long train," he confessed. "Take men for example. We don't have to do all of that. If it was left up to us, we would just get married."

Adriana was too nervous to respond; her mind was going in a million directions. There was nothing but silence as they took the ride to the ground floor.

Marvin took his position as "protector" of the princess as the elevator pinged to let them know they had arrived in the lobby. He stepped off the elevator and extended his right elbow once again to the young lady who stole the other part of his heart. He was still holding her train.

Adriana noticed a few people who had stepped aside as they began to walk through the hotel lobby.

"So beautiful," she heard a female voice whisper.

"Thank you," Adriana said in the direction of the voice.

Just as they were reaching the exit door a man entered. He wore a black, tailed tuxedo and rolled, brim top hat.

"My lady, it is a little windy today," the driver informed her as he offered her a scarf.

Adriana knew the scarf all too well. It was one Grandma Gina used to cover her hair at one of her cousins' outdoor weddings.

"Thank you," Adriana said with a smile. She should have expected as much because Grandma Gina was most astute when it came to all things' etiquette and protecting that which she valued the most.

On instinct, Marvin carefully retrieved the broach he had been given just in case something needed to be held in place.

"Your grandmother wore this cape on your mother's wedding day," Marvin informed his daughter.

"I thought you and mama were married in May," Adriana said with confusion.

"It was early May," Marvin affirmed. "It was cold and windy that day. Today somewhat reminds me of that day."

Marvin was trying to place the scarf over his daughter's head.

"Dad, be careful with my hair."

Courtney, one of Adriana's cousins in crime, had crafted the perfect hairstyle. Adriana's long, dark, brown hair was pinned in a messy bun with wisps of curls framing her face and dangling down her back.

"No worries," Marvin comforted his daughter. "We don't have to use the scarf if you don't want to. The canopy has been raised, so it should block most of the wind." He lowered his arms.

Adriana looked through the last set of double doors in search of her carriage. She saw a white carriage adorned with white roses and yellow daffodils. The canopy was raised just as Marvin had promised. The driver had made it to the carriage and was opening the doors and rolling out the steps. The interior of the carriage was upholstered in a silk, velvet, burgundy fabric.

CONFUSION, COMPASSION, CONFESSION - 13

The driver aided Adriana into the carriage by holding her right hand while Marvin secured her on the left. The driver directed Adriana to her seat and adjusted the chapel train to allow Marvin to enter. Then, he softly situated the train again to protect it from Marvin's shoes.

"Ready, My Lady," the driver asked with enthusiasm.

"Ready."

The driver turned to Marvin, "And you, Sir? Are you ready?"

"I think I am," Marvin answered, realizing how loaded the question really was.

The driver finished securing the father and his daughter before returning to his perch. He knew how important this moment was for the bride. The dream of being Cinderella and Princess Diana lived in every bride who sought his services. It was his duty to make sure they felt just as important on their wedding day as they saw Diana on hers.

The driver gently lifted, then snapped the reins. The horses followed their command. Adriana braced herself as they left the covered entrance of the hotel. The driver slowly guided his horses onto 4th Street.

The March wind was not as strong as it had been a few weeks ago; however, it made Adriana lift her hands to protect her hair.

"You will be okay," Marvin said to reassure her. "I'm sure the driver knows what he is doing. This is not his first time having to deal with a bride and wind."

Believing her father's reassurance, Adriana pressed her back on the soft velvet for the short ride. The trot to the intersection of Tryon Street made Adriana look up at one of her favorite bistros.

The light turned green. The horses' steps reminded both Adriana and Marvin about the life changes that were ahead of them.

A turn onto Poplar Street broke the silence between them.

"Daddy, how did you feel the day you married Mama?"

"I was excited. I was nervous. I was ready to get it over with."

"Did you have any doubts?"

"None. Your mother is a rare find," he affirmed with confidence and a sense of remorse.

"Do you ever wish that things had worked out differently?" she probed.

"Your mother is truly a one in a million finds, Adriana. We were young, and I did not know what I had in her until it was too late," Marvin responded without answering the question.

Adriana thought she understood her father's answer. If he had admitted to making a mistake, then he would have to admit that her half-siblings were mistakes. She decided to accept her father's answer as it stood.

She had done the calculations and knew that her parents had to get married when they did. Otherwise, her father would've finished college before making that commitment, and her mother would've earned her degree. Something inside of her told her that fifty-seven-year-old Marvin was a much different man.

"We're here," the driver notified.

The announcement made Adriana look to her right. They had arrived at the Mint Museum. She loved all things art. It had been her dream to be married in a museum since seeing the King Tut exhibit when she was in middle school. She looked at the steps then took a deep breath.

Just as the pharaohs in ancient Egypt had been laid to rest in the great pyramids to journey to them to their after lives, she was on her way to lay to rest her past and journey into her future.

"My lady," the driver offered his hand to help her exit the carriage. He joined her father in situating the train for her assent to the entrance.

Adriana looked behind her then took four steps forward. She

checked her train one last time before returning her attention to what was awaiting her.

Standing at the top of the stairs were members of the bride's wedding party. They were all smiles and full of joy. The overhang of the building was protecting them from the wind that was beginning to pick up a little speed.

Adriana turned to the driver, "What's your name, sir?" she asked.

"William," the man answered.

"Thank you, William," she said in appreciation of his help.

"You are one of the most beautiful brides I have had the pleasure of serving," William replied with the tip of his hat. "God be with you and your man. May you be blessed with healthy children and peace in your lives."

Jordan, one of Adriana's older brothers had made his way down the stairs to help his sister up.

"He's waiting for you," Jordan said to Adriana as he extended his left hand to her.

Adriana's heart leaped and a smile formed on her face without her ever noticing what was happening to her.

A small gust of wind swept across her face. The curl that framed the right side of her face made its way into her mouth. On instinct, she reached for the ornate bun on her head as she blew the curl away.

"Come on," Marvin commanded his children as he led the way up the stairs.

The bridesmaids and matron of honor had returned to the inside of the museum by the time Adriana had ascended the stairs. Audrey, the wedding director, greeted her as soon as she stepped inside the building. She immediately directed her to the bridal suite.

Audrey directed the wedding party to wait outside the bridal suite until she directed them to move. Once inside the bridal suite, Courtney gave Adriana's hair and make-up a touch-up.

"It's not as bad as I thought it would be," Courtney said.

"Now," that distinctive voice that knew exactly how to calm any anxiety resonated through the room.

Adriana turned to see her Grandma Gina holding a tiara. Tears formed in her eyes.

"None of that; you will mess up from make-up," the matriarch of the White family said.

Adriana nodded her head in obedience.

"My grandmother had this tiara made for me for my wedding," Grandma Gina began. "Her name was Pearl Anabelle."

Adriana noticed the pearls that were in the tiara.

"Pearl's great-great-grandmother had been a countess. I am passing this tiara down to you now because I want you to remember this part of who you are."

Adriana returned to her seat. She was excited to see her other favorite grandmother because her health had been failing her.

"It is important for you to remember who you are. Never forget who you are," ordered the octogenarian who was beginning to show signs of osteoporosis.

"The two diamonds in the center are family heirlooms. It was a secret my grandmother shared with me, and now it is our secret."

"Why didn't you give it to Mama?"

"Both of my daughters borrowed it for their weddings. I am giving it you because you are my oldest granddaughter."

"Is the fur mines to keep, too?"

"I believe the fur is yours to keep, too. We know you will take excellent care of them and give them to your daughter or granddaughter someday," was spoken with a smile and admiration.

Grandma Gina has always admired the shape of Adriana's nostrils. Whenever she looked at them, she thought about a heart. She slowly turned then left the room, giving the young ladies waiting outside permission to return.

"Are you ready?" Cilicia asked.

"More than ready." Excitement turned into anxiety. In less than an hour her life would metamorphose into a missus.

Courtney took the veil out of its bag. She and Cilicia carefully fanned the veil out to reveal the scalloped edges with lace embroidery and pearls.

Courtney secured the veil below the bun that perfectly accented the tiara. Audrey joined the maid and matron as they situated the veil to extend below the train.

"No crying," Courtney reminded Adriana.

"No crying," Adriana repeated.

Courtney did one last check of the make-up for any imperfections before turning to Cilicia and Audrey, "We're good to go."

Audrey led the way outside of the bridal suite.

Adriana was left alone with her thoughts for only a few seconds. She briefly thought about her senior year of college before she was interrupted by the opening of the door.

"We have to go now." That was Audrey's assistant, who led Adriana to the grand hall.

They arrived just as the ringbearer, Gavin's nephew, stood in place. Adriana looked to her right and saw her dad unfold his arms. He was prepared to escort his daughter down the aisle.

As soon as the pianist hit the F note, tears began to stream out of Adriana's eyes.

"I told Gavin I was not going to cry," to whispered to herself.

Marvin offered his daughter his handkerchief.

Adriana felt her dad's lead down the aisle. She slowly joined him. Tears were still streaming. She had promised Courtney she would not cry. She had told Gavin she would not cry. It had been an entire minute before the tears stopped. She could finally see what was ahead of her.

Adriana reached the row where her mother sat. She stood in

place until her mother joined her on her left. Then the trio approached the platform where the minister stood.

Adriana's eyes met Gavin's. It had been three days since she last looked into those eyes. Three days had not changed the look he gave her the very first time she realized he was in love with her. He smiled. She smiled back.

"Dearly beloved, we have gathered here today...," Reverend Sanderson began.

"Marriage is a covenant, a trinity that is established by God, man, and woman...," he continued.

Adriana's mind was lost in time until she heard Gavin say, "I do."

"Do you promise to love, honor, cherish, and protect her, forsaking all others and holding only unto her forevermore?" Gavin was questioned by the minister.

Another, "I do," came from Gavin as he looked at Reverend Sanderson then to Adriana.

"Adriana, do you take Gavin to be your husband?" Reverend Sanderson asked.

"I do," was her answer.

"Adriana, do you promise to love, honor, cherish, and protect him, forsaking all others and holding only unto him forevermore?" Reverend Sanderson put the questions to the bride.

Again, she answered, "I do."

"Who gives this woman to be married to this man?" was the next question.

"We do," Regenia and Marvin responded in unison. Then they took their seats.

Adriana and Gavin proceeded through the traditional, Christian, wedding vows and exchanged wedding rings. They knelled for prayer.

"God, our father, you have brought together Gavin and Adriana before each of us. We ask that you bless this union and strengthen them as they continue to grow in your goodness and grace. Bless their love and remind them each day that you are the head of their lives. Gavin has been placed as the head of his family before you and your son, Jesus the Christ. Lead him, oh God, direct his path so that the family bond shall remain strong before you. Bless their unborn children. Guide Gavin and Adriana as parents now and forever. Keep them safe and strengthen them to avoid the temptations that will come their way," Reverend Sanderson said.

Adriana felt the olive oil cross her head; she slightly opened her left eye to witness the same for Gavin.

"For now, and forever more. Amen!" Reverend Sanderson conclude his prayer.

On cue they returned to a standing position.

"We will now share communion with this couple, their parents, and grandparents," announced the minister.

Unleavened bread and red wine were distributed.

Reverend Sanderson turned to the groom. "Gavin, you are to love Adriana as Christ loved the Church."

He turned to the bride. "Adriana, you are to follow Gavin just as the disciplines followed Jesus so long as God continues to be the head of his life."

He lifted his bread in front of him and slightly above his head.

"Let us eat together."

Gavin and Adriana lifted their bread then placed it in their mouths.

He continued. "Gavin, Christ gave his body so that we might be forgiven for our sins. This wine is representative of the sacrifices Christ made for us. It is also symbolizing your responsibility to Adriana and your unborn children."

"Adriana, Christs followers were responsible for going forth into the world spreading the good news about his life. Like the followers of Christ, Gavin will need you to be his greatest supporter," Reverend Sanderson commanded.

He lifted his wine glass in front of him slightly above his head.

"Let us drink together."

Gavin and Adriana lifted their wine glasses then drank the wine.

Adriana looked at Gavin, the man who had become her husband. He gazed into her eyes.

Reverend Sanderson motioned from them to face their guests.

"Ladies and gentlemen, I present to you Mr. & Mrs. Gavin Douglass Matthews. You may kiss your bride, Sir," Reverend Sanderson said.

Gavin reached for Adriana's hand. He leaned into her face then gave her the kiss that had sparked magic into her; the kind of magic that she had dreamed of but never knew existed. He looked into her eyes then said, "Mrs. Adriana La'Rosa Regenia Matthews." Adriana's heart melted. Together they turned to face their guests. Gavin gave Adriana's hand a slight squeeze to let her know she had been joined with her forever life partner.

One of Gavin's friends from college sang "The Most Beautiful Girl in the World" by Prince as they waved to their guests on their way down the aisle. Gavin had requested the song because he wanted Adriana to know that it was her inner beauty that made her outer beauty most beautiful. It was the outer beauty that attracted him, but her inner beauty is what gave her his name.

As they reached the end of the aisle, Audrey motioned for the couple to move to the terrace where the cocktail party was held. The wedding party followed.

"Get a quick snack," she announced. "Pictures in 15 minutes."

3

Cilicia

Cilicia rushed to the patio. She scanned the area for food. She had eaten an early breakfast because she was second on the list for hair and makeup and only snacked for lunch. Her stomach was telling her that food needed to come soon.

She spotted Sheraton, the young lady Winston introduced everyone to at the Christmas party. She mouthed to her, "food."

Sheraton pointed to Cilicia's left. "Thanks," she waved then hurried to her left.

She found the hors d'oeuvres. She made her way to the shrimp and chocolate covered strawberries. Just as she was about to get punch, Justus appeared by her side.

"What are you doing out here? You heard the lady say fifteen minutes before pictures."

"I am hungry and was beginning to feel a little sick, Justus. Do you want me to pass out?" Cilicia answered.

He firmly gripped her forearm then led her away from the

punch. "People are waiting on us," he said with the same firmness he was using to grip her arm.

She tried to snatch her arm out of his grip, but it was too powerful. She wiggled a little more.

"I still have time," she pleaded with her husband.

"I don't want us to be late."

"You can go back in. I will be right there."

"I'll wait."

Cilicia quickly returned to the punch and snatched the one in the front. She gulped it down in four swallows. She knew how important this day was to Adriana; she remembered her own wedding. She also knew Justus always needed to appear powerful and in control in front of his friends and colleagues, so she played along.

Justus escorted his wife of three years back inside. Adriana and Gavin were taking pictures with their grandparents. Cilicia tried to relax herself a little knowing she was not holding anyone up. Justus tugged her skirt to remind her to straighten up her posture. Without hesitation, she assumed the pose she used when she won Miss South Carolina.

Although she felt exhausted from the weekend, she made sure to have her pageant smile on for pictures. Justus's tug was still embedded in her mind, so the pageant pose remained.

Cilicia was very self-conscious during dinner. Darius, the groomsman she was paired with, was very talkative and friendly. Engaging in conversation with him would certainly cause Justus to erupt when they got in the car, so she tried her best to limit the number of words she spoke to him.

As soon as the father-daughter dance was over, Cilicia made her way to the patio. She searched for familiar, female faces from college. During the course of her search, she found Sheraton who was standing alone looking at the Charlotte skyline. Cilicia felt a sense of relief when she saw her.

She approached the petite, sandy body with the asymmetrical bob haircut. Something about her made Cilicia think about Left Eye.

"I didn't get a chance to talk with you at the Christmas party," Cilicia said to her.

"It was fine. I knew everyone was very busy," Sheraton replied.

"Are you from Charlotte?"

"No; I am from Maryland."

"How did you meet Winston?"

"I met him at my brother's party last summer. They're fraternity brothers."

"Soo," Cilicia began, raising her eyebrows with a slight smile, "Winston has been keeping secrets."

"I didn't know I was supposed to be a secret," Sheraton shyly answered.

"We haven't seen you until Christmas."

"I've been busy with school."

"School?"

"I'm in my senior year of college, so I am only around during the holidays."

"Okay; that explains why Winston hasn't been around much."

"Yeah, he comes to me on weekends," Sheraton admitted.

Cilicia began to feel a little uneasy. She focused on the images that were emerging in the window. She looked over the left shoulder and saw the six feet, rich caramel physique being trailed by someone equal in height with amber skin. Both men had tapelines that tapered into their mustaches and beards. Justus's hardened pectoralis was no longer hidden by his buttoned, tuxedo jacket.

Cilicia smiled at her husband then reached for his hand. She looked at Winston. "I see you've been keeping secrets."

Justus looked down at her.

"Nobody's keeping secrets," Winston said. "You'll see more of her when she finishes school."

"Justus, do you remember Sheraton from the Christmas party? She was Winston's date," Cilicia was trying to refresh her husband's memory.

"Yes; I remember her," Justus acknowledged while extending his hand to Sheraton. "How've you been?"

"I'm good," Sheraton answered. She looked up at Winston and smiled.

"This is my first time in the center city of Charlotte. It's a pretty city," Sheraton said.

"Yeah; it is a pretty city," Justus agreed.

Cilicia looked out the window one last time. The image she had seen in the window and the way it moved, told her she would have a long ride home.

"Sheraton, I hope to see you soon," Cilicia said as she prepared to leave.

"I know I will you see you soon," Sheraton replied. "Maybe you can show me some of the best places around here."

"Adriana and I will plan a girls' day and invite you."

"That would be great," Sheraton said.

Justus looked at Sheraton then Winston, "I'll see you Monday," he said to Winston.

Winston shook his head, "Monday it is."

Cilicia reached for Justus's arm and pulled him closer than she and Darius had been earlier. She knew her husband; he had been watching every move her body made for signs of her "getting too comfortable" with someone else. She wanted to let him know who she belonged to; she needed to ease his tensions before getting into the car.

The couple left the museum with Justus leading the way.

Still Having and Still Holding

Still having and holding to what God put together;
The promise we made to love forever;
The healing you gave this broken heart;
The revival I gave when you were torn apart;
The enemies we've faced; the strength we've gain;
The faith we've held onto is what keeps me sane.

4

Dear Diary

Dear Diary,
I feel numb, paralyzed. I have a lump in my throat and need it to come up. I haven't felt this way in over twenty years. The last time I felt this way I knew I was in a do or die situation. I knew that if I didn't leave, I would die. Sitting here now reminds me of that day. The day I had to make a decision on how I was going to live.

It all seems like yesterday when I came home to celebrate my nineteenth birthday with Courtney and my friends from high school. We were dressed in our favorite outfits like we were members of TLC. I had on an emerald shirt and hipster jeans with my belly button showing off. Mona and Courtney were dressed the same but in red and orange shirts. You couldn't tell us we weren't Left Eye, T-Boz, and Chilli; we were crazy, sexy, and cool.

The day had been simply perfect because we were all home from college. We had gone to a house party and felt like nothing could stop our dreams from coming true. We were singing "Kick Your Game" when we got back to Byron's house. Oh, that was such a great time.

Byron acted as if everything was okay. He had always been one of our biggest fans when we were in high school; he encouraged us all the time. He fixed us drinks, and we reminisced about our senior year of high school. He even talked about his senior year of high school, too. As soon as Mona and Courtney left, everything turned dark.

Byron punched me in the stomach. I lost my breath because it took me off guard. Then he pulled my ponytail and punched my face. He kept hitting me in my face and stomach so that I could not remember what was happening to me. All I could remember was him spitting on me and saying, "You bitch!" It took a while for me to get myself together. I didn't know what to do, so I went to a hotel for the night.

Byron kept calling my phone. I wouldn't answer. I didn't know what to do. I didn't want anyone to know what had happened, so I texted Bryon and told him I was okay. When Mona and Courtney wanted to hang out the next day, I told them that I had a hangover from the night before. I had lied to them before, but this time was a little different. I could see in Byron's eyes that he had more hate for me than love. This was not the same hand around my neck or slap in the face that he used to do. This was something different.

I texted Byron the next day and told him it was over. I warned that if he called my parents, I would tell them everything about the abuse. He said he was sorry and begged me to give him another chance. He said he would change, but I didn't believe him. Being away at college gave me courage to think about my safety. Knowing that I had options in life and realizing that I would not be returning home after I graduated helped me more than I realized.

I wanted to release myself from carrying the secret of Bryon's abuse. I wanted the freedom that my roommate had. I wanted to be able to go to parties or talk to guys who talked to me without feeling like I was cheating on Bryon. I wanted to be able to just be free!

I have also wanted to be free of this secret. This is the first time I have told anyone about that night. The first time I allowed myself to remember it.

I want to say more, but I can't. I want this lump to leave my throat, but I don't know how to speak the words. Writing them is impossible, too.

From one prison to another; from one pain to another; from one tear to another – freedom is just an illusion.

5

Seventeen Years Later

Seventeen years had passed since her wedding. The long, layered bob Adriana wore in her late twenties was a half foot shorter and a little thinner.

She shifted her hips in the seat to lean a little closer to the mirror. She rested her elbows onto the built-in vanity.

She inspected her eyes for wrinkles. She could see some lines beginning to emerge.

"Mama always said I had a few wrinkles around my eyes when I was born," she said to herself. "Hopefully these are the same lines I was born with."

Then she checked for the wrinkles in her forehead.

"How long have they been here?"

Adriana exhaled then leaned her back against her chair. She sat in contemplation. She rose to the edge of her seat.

"You are less than two years from your forty-fifth birthday. Of course, you are going to have wrinkles that were not present when you got married," she continued the conversation with herself.

She gently rubbed the lines then attempted to stretch them out.

"Lines are a natural part of the aging process," she reminded herself.

She stretched them again.

"I guess I had better start getting Botox injections if I want them to go away."

Adriana rose from her chair. She turned to inspect her naked body. She massaged her neck that had shortened since her wedding. She twirled her head then leaned it from side to side.

"Aahh," she gasped.

She examined her breasts that had always been lighter than her face and neck. She lifted the C-cups and pushed them inward. She turned to her left then her right.

"These puppies still have a little perk to them," she said to herself as she bounced them up and down.

She pinched her nipples between her forefinger and thumb while massaging her breasts. She closed her eyes and enjoyed the moment.

Adriana glided her right hand from her chest to her torso. Although her waistline had increased a few inches, there was no evidence of stretch marks on her abdomen. She had taken great care of her skin during her pregnancies because she wanted to look great in a bikini.

She turned to her right to inspect her hips and buttocks. She rubbed her hips that had widened just a little. She rubbed her hand on her butt; it still had its nice, round shape.

She faced forward in the mirror again. She tilted her head to the right and then to the left. She moved from side to side still inspecting her body. Hip to waist ratio was still good.

Again, she moved her right hand to her torso. She slipped it down to her pubic hair.

Adriana widened her legs then stopped her middle finger on her clitoris. She slowly glided her middle and ring fingers to place her clitoris between them. Her hand moved up and down.

She grasped her left breast. She lifted the breast to her mouth. She licked her nipple.

She moved her middle finger into her vagina then to her clitoris. She continued to relieve the stress that was causing her to have sleepless nights.

She took her finger out of her vagina and placed it in her mouth.

She walked to her bathtub and climbed in. She reached for her pillow then laid her back on the porcelain.

Adriana positioned her right leg on the edge of the tub. She reached for the bottle of oil and quirted some on her middle finger.

She massaged her clitoris and pinched her nipple. She slid her finger into her vagina. She felt the wetness increase in her body. Her clitoris had grown bigger.

Her movements became quicker, and she applied more pressure. She closed her eyes and released the energy that was in her body. It had been over twenty years since she had taken herself to seventh heaven.

6

September, Awareness Month

"Just use your key when you get here," Adriana instructed her mother while pulling her workout pants over her hips. She reached for her blue wicking shirt, knowing it would come in handy later in the morning.

She abruptly opened her bedroom door then jetted down the hallway. Still pulling her shirt down to her hips, she rapped on the door, slightly pushed it open.

"Your grandmother is here."

Adriana quickly surveyed her daughter. Hair – check; attire –check; shoes – check. The inspection assured her Ariadne would meet her grandmother's approval. She backed out of the room then went next door. Double tap before entering. No one was there.

She walked to the mezzanine and leaned as far as she could. She had her answer. Nicklous was bolting towards the front door.

Adriana stood watch over her son as he unlatched the two locks to give entry to his maternal matriarch.

"Grandma," he said with excitement, extending his arms for a big hug.

A hug was given back with a gentle, "Hello, Grandson," that was loaded with pride and joy.

Adriana stood in admiration of her mother. She had hoped that she, too, would look like her children's mother when she became a grandmother.

Regenia stood right at five feet. There were no visible gray hairs in the seventy-year-old; her hair was still black. She was still size eight and had no signs of osteoporosis. She bounced out of view along with her youngest grandson.

Adriana knew all was well as long as Nicklous was entertaining his grandmother, so she returned to her room to finish her hair.

She leaned into the full-length mirror. There was no need for make-up today, so that wouldn't be an issue. She turned to her left and rubbed her hands down both sides of her body. She turned to her right and did the same. She turned to the back to make sure there were no visible panty lines.

Downward dog pose; "Yes!" Adriana said out loud.

Warrior 1; warrior 2; triangle; reverse warrior; downward dog; exhale.

A quick look at the rear again; rub down on the belly; last check of hair.

Adriana took a deep breath then went into the hallway.

A double tap on Ariadne's door, "Your grandmother's here."

By the time Adriana arrived downstairs, Nicklous was already updating his grandmother on the important things in his life – his grades and his football schedule.

"I got Mama to print my schedule for you," Nicklous said as he handed her the important paper.

Regenia received the paper from her grandson. She inspected the dates and times.

"I see you have two eight o'clock games here. Am I expected to be at those, too?"

"Grandma," Nicklous said titling his head to right, "you can stay in the bedroom here. You don't have to drive home any night."

"Hello, Mother," came Adriana's greeting as she met her mother's eyes.

"Hello, Daughter. Nicklous has given me a copy of his football schedule and put the dates and times in my calendar," the grandmother said with admiration. "He makes sure I don't miss anything."

"What do you have planned for today?" Adriana inquired.

"The apple orchard, of course. Then whatever movie the kids want to see."

"Let your granddaughter decide," injected Nicklous's voice. "She's one who likes to be the boss."

Adriana handed her mother a cup of coffee. Regenia slowly raised the cup to her lips. Coffee with Adriana was one of her life's pleasures.

"This is good. What blend is this?"

"It's a Costa Rican blend one of my students brought me from her summer vacation," Adriana answered. "I thought you would like it."

Adriana sat Nicklous's plate in front of him then did the same for her mother. She placed her plate on the bar in front of her mother and son.

"Only three plates?" Regenia asked.

"Adriadne likes to fix her own breakfast," Nicklous answered. "She likes to eat her fruit and cheese. She may or may not eat a bagel," he continued just before biting into his own.

Ariadne bounced into the kitchen. Her almond shaped eyes met her grandmother. She had no control over the reflex that displayed the pink bands in her mouth.

"Grandma," came the greeting along with a lean into the frame that was not as firm as it was fourteen years ago when it first held her in its arms.

The arms extended. On cue, Ariadne kicked her left leg in front of her. She extended her arms to her sides then placed her fingers near her waistline. She slowly glided them towards her feet. Then she stretched them out and did a Y pose as if she had finished a cheerleading routine. She placed her hands on her waist then twirled around.

"Did you need to do all that?" Nicklous questioned.

"Mind yo' business," Ariadne answered her brother with a snap of her head.

Adriana leaned onto the counter and took the last bite of her bagel.

"No fighting you two," she said to her children.

Placing her bagel into the toaster, Ariadne began updating her grandmother on all the important things – grades, dance team, and orchestra.

Adriana walked to the sofa where Nicklous was sitting. She rubbed his hair. She went to Ariadne and tapped her on her hips.

"Mom, you know, I'm getting too old for that," Ariadne protested.

Adriana grabbed her purse, keys, and laptop.

"Why do you need your laptop?" Regenia questioned. "I thought you were going to a race."

"I am going to a race, Mom. Cilicia called and asked to do lunch, so I might have time to grade some papers along the way."

"Is everything okay?"

Placing everything on the counter, Adriana decided to do some arm stretches while she answered her mother's questions.

"The normal things I guess."

"The normal things?"

"The normal things." Adriana looked up at her mother with the, "You know what adult life is like," look as she twisted into her left side.

Adriana did one last set of jumping jacks.

She turned to her mother, "Thanks for everything, Mom."

* * *

Adriana spotted the check-in table. She tucked her keys inside the hide-away pocket of pants and placed her phone in her left pocket.

"Good morning, Blair," she greeted her friend from church. "I didn't know you would be here."

"My mom asked me to come at the last minute," Blair said. "Her association had a few spots left for volunteers, so I came to help."

Adriana was among the early arrivals. Months had passed since Adriana had been to church, so she and Blair gave updates on their lives.

Blair was still working her part-time position at an accounting firm and was considering a full-time, work-from-home position. Her sons had earned their driver's licenses, so Blair had more free time on her hands. Her daughter was a member of the golf team, which made her husband proud.

Then Blair questioned Adriana on how her children and Gavin were doing. Adriana told her that things were still the same.

"We've got to get together soon," Blair said. "We didn't spend any time together this summer."

Adriana promised to make time for them to get together before the holiday season. She got her assignment and materials then proceeded to her location.

Monica, one of her students, was already in their spot. "Good morning, Mrs. Matthews," Monica greeted as she extended her arms to help Adriana place the materials on their table.

"Good morning, Monica," Adriana greeted the future teacher who was also president of the club Adriana sponsored at school.

"Have you started grading our essays?" Monica asked.

"I hope to get them done this weekend," Adriana said.

Monica moved the materials to the chairs. She unfolded their club's tablecloth and stretched it out on the table.

"Sylvia Plath and 'Lady Lazarus' are very interesting," Monica began talking as she worked on setting up the table. "I have a friend who attempted suicide. The EMTs had to give him two doses of that drug to bring him back."

Adriana was a bit perplexed; she had not prepared herself for such an intense conversation. She had needed the crispness of the late September morning to clear her mind of her reality; that was part of the reason why she loved doing the Recovery Walks. Although they were on the last Saturday of Recovery Awareness Month, her mind did not want to think of substance abuse or suicide until she began reading her students' essays.

"How is your friend now?" Adriana inquired.

"He still feels guilt over his brother's suicide. He sort of blames himself because he said his brother told him what he was thinking about doing, but he didn't believe him."

"Your friend is carrying a heavy burden," Adriana acknowledged.

Monica's lips dropped from being an almost smile. She lowered her eyes. She shifted her weight from her right leg to her left leg then back again. She rubbed her hands over the tablecloth to straighten out the creases.

Adriana stood still to brace herself for what might be coming next, even the admission from Monica that she was the friend she was talking about. She knew she needed to become the comforter

Monica was pleading for. Her eighteen years in education had taught her a lot about teenagers.

Monica looked up at Adriana. "It was my brother who attempted suicide."

"So it your brother who committed suicide," Adriana said to gain clarity.

"Not really. Frederick is my half-brother, and Lawrence was HIS brother."

Adriana rubbed Monica on her back; she did not know what else to do. She could see the child needed comfort and was trying her best to be the presence the child needed in her life.

"I am here because I want my brother to recover, Mrs. Matthews," Monica continued with tears in her voice. "I want him to live. My family acts as if there is nothing wrong with marijuana; they act like it's okay. But I know what my brother told me. He said that eventually, marijuana made him want to do other things. So, he began to put cocaine in his cigarettes."

Monica cried in Adriana's arms. "So many things happen to people when they are young that they use drugs to cope. That's what Frederick and Lawrence did. I don't want to be a Lazarus, Mrs. Matthews, because sometimes people don't come back."

* * *

Adriana had joined Monica on the track and briskly walked the three miles because she could sense the young lady needed to talk. Monica had shared that her family had generational curses she didn't want to be a part of. The child had reported to the walk because she needed to clear her head from last night's party.

Adriana shook her head. "That's the hardest part about being a teacher; you can't rescue them from their own lives," she thought to herself.

As she refueled her body, she continued to think about the five-k conversation she had with Monica. The young lady seemed to be enthralled with the life of the poet whose work they had recently read. She had wondered how close to his edge her brother had been before he needed to be brought back. Thinking about their conversation was preparing Adriana for the essays she was about to grade. She wondered how much of her essay Monica had shared with her.

She had chosen the French Quarter because it was right across the street from the park. Parking in this area of Charlotte was limited, so she felt lucky to be able to park in front of the restaurant.

She gazed out the window. A lot had changed downtown in the past twenty years. Romare Bearden Park wasn't there when she and Gavin married, but it had become one of her favorite places to relax. Her phone flashed.

"I am sitting at the table by the second window," she texted.

She motioned for her waitress. She mouthed, "Box" while pointing to her wings.

"It's Saturday, Girl, and the Summer has cooled off, so what's with the lines in your forehead?" Adriana greeted Cilicia as she sat down opposite her.

Adriana had taken notice of Cilicia's pacing as she approached the building. Her steeled body and sunken jaws told Adriana that Cilicia was on a mission.

"It's hard to cool off something that has set you on fire," Cilicia said with determination in her eyes.

"Let's talk, so I can help you cool off," Adriana said, hoping it was not going to take long; she didn't want to lose her focus on what she needed to accomplish over the weekend.

"How was the race?" asked Cilicia, who had declined the invitation to join the race.

"Refreshing; I really needed that before spending the rest of the weekend grading essays," Adriana was happy to inform. "I have to take advantage of my mom being here and spending time with the kids."

"Count your blessings," Cilicia said. One thing she had envied in Adriana's life was the fact that her mother was willing to come lend a helping hand whenever her daughter needed it.

"This is their weekend to do the apple orchard. Ariadne really didn't want to go, so we'll have to see how it goes next year. Where are Alexus and Evian today?"

"Band is doing a camp this weekend, so they are both there," Cilicia answered with a softened jaw.

Adriana was happy to see Cilicia was beginning to relax. They talked about their teaching experiences and how much students in both high school and community college had changed over the years.

"Has Alexus been thinking about any colleges in particular this year?" Adriana asked.

"She's been talking about graduating early," Cilicia answered with frustration.

"Graduating early?"

"She says she is ready to leave home and begin her own life."

"Has she been researching colleges and careers?"

"Her heart has always been set on Carolina. Last year she visited Howard with the Tri-County HBCU Alliance; she had not mentioned the school since her visit. She plans to do the Common Application next month while some colleges are not requiring their usual application fee," Cilicia said.

"How does Justus feel about her wanting to graduate early?" Adriana inquired.

"We haven't talked with him about it," Cilicia answered lowering her eyes and head.

"Why not?"

The lines in Cilicia's forehead became more pronounced. Her eyes became watery; her left bottom lip pulled slightly in.

"Things are not good between us right now."

"What do you mean?"

Cilicia reached into her purse and pulled out her tablet. She carefully unlocked it, then she slid it over to Adriana.

"Let me show you." She scrolled through pictures to help Adriana understand why things were not going well for them.

Adriana looked up at her. "What is this?" she asked pointing to a picture.

"You see it."

"I am talking about this one." Adriana scrolled back to the picture to make sure she saw what she thought she saw.

"I never liked Blair, Adriana. I told you that. Now you see why."

Adriana's face stiffened. "We made a promise to never do this."

Cilicia continued to scroll. Adriana looked down again. She stood up and gathered her laptop case.

"Adriana, wait," Cilicia said trying to stop Adriana from what she was about to do.

"Why would you show this to me?" Adriana asked with tears in her eyes and frustration in her voice.

"Because you need to know just like I needed to know," Cilicia said.

"Know what exactly?"

"That Gavin has been lying to you just like Justus has been lying to me."

"Cilicia, we made a promise to never do this to each other," Adriana said with frustration and disappointment.

"No; we promised to never carry each other to a place where we saw it happening."

With those words, Adriana left a twenty on the table. She shot

Cilicia one last look as if she could kill her, then she left her friend to deal with her own thoughts just as she had to process her own.

7

Pushing Boundaries

Adriana was sitting at her vanity in deep thought. The winds from Ophelia had blown through downtown Charlotte and helped cool the fire that was raging in her.

Cilicia had crossed a boundary that had been set since their sophomore year of college. They made the agreement after Keelah, one of the girls in the junior class at their college, had been stabbed by her boyfriend's other girl; Keelah's friends had taken her to the spot where her boyfriend was hanging out with the other girl to confront them; they had no idea that the other girl had more survival skills than Keelah; she almost lost her life over the injuries. It was that situation that created the pact to never set each other up to be hurt over a man.

Cilicia had encroached on territory that was sacred to their friendship. They had always promised to protect each other from things that could threaten them in any way whatsoever.

Sure, people had come to Adriana with tales of Justus; however, she never felt the need to share them with Cilicia. Those things that could have and would have led her to a place of unhappiness. Adriana had decided to allow Cilicia to share with her what she wanted her to know, and even then, Adriana was careful not to offer her advice on what to do. She didn't want to do anything that would not be to her friend's benefit.

Seventeen years of bliss had mostly been her experience with Gavin. Adriana's friends and co-workers admired and complimented her on the success of her marriage, which had been the source of her pride. Those were also the things that made her believe in Gavin and what they shared.

"Sure, I would get married," some people would say to Gavin and her, "if my marriage could be like yours."

But had she been lying to herself? She was viewing life through rose-colored glasses. Was she living in a glass house that was about to be shattered?

Adriana was often an ear and advisor to her friends and associates. They would call her or stop her while she was shopping or running and ask for advice on how to handle situations in their marriages and relationships. She would give the same or similar advice she had been given by her father and uncles.

"Give him a little time. Your husband has a lot on his shoulders. Every day he is facing a world that does not want to accept him," was the advice Adriana often heard from the men in her family.

"Remember why you married him in the first place," was another popular one she would use when she got tired of hearing the complaints.

"Our men are still trying to adjust to living in a white-collar world," was other advice given to her and that she gave. "That transition is not always easy. Be patient with him."

The invention of social media and chat groups had given her some relief from being an unlicensed therapist for many people.

Even her best friend, who herself was a psychologist, needed her to play the role of therapist from time to time.

Adriana rose from her dressing table. It was her favorite place to retreat to when she was contemplating things going on in her life. Rarely was she doubting Gavin and their relationship. She had never had a reason to question the security of her marriage.

"Why don't you look and see what you find," Cilicia had said to her. "You might be surprised."

"BITCH! Why would you do this to me?" Adriana asked Cilicia, who was not there to answer.

"I would never do this to you! NEVER!" she exclaimed as she threw her left arm towards the mirror with her pointed index finger.

Rage had swelled in Adriana. Rage that she had felt only twice in her life – the day she returned to Byron's apartment and the day she put sugar in Jamie's gas tank. They had crossed boundaries, too. They had caused Adriana to feel powerless over her life; they had tried to destroy her beauty that brought out her beast.

She looked down at her wedding rings. Being with Gavin had made her forget that part of herself, her life. She knew her range for Bryon could've resulted in something more serious than it had been. If the fire had been ignited, her life would've taken a different direction.

Adriana's chest moved in and out; the pace of her breathing slowed. She put both hands on the marble as she looked in the mirror. She had been stabbed in the back by friends in the past, but this was the first time she had been stabbed in her heart. It was one thing for Cilicia to show her pictures of a man holding his dick that she said was Gavin's. The nerve of her to show pictures of man having his dick sucked and saying it was Gavin's was another story.

Adriana looked at her growing rage. That beast was still in there.

She searched her mind and examined her feelings. She thought about her Grandma Gina and the times her grandmother seemed distant. She remembered the music her grandmother used to play during those times. Adriana picked up her phone and found a concerto. She never knew what had happened in her grandmother's life that would make her go there, but today she understood. Whatever IT was, IT was taking Adriana there, too. She needed her fangs to go back in.

Adriana faced the closet she shared with her husband. The closet had been designed to her specifications: a dresser, cabinets, wall to ceiling storage units on each side, and an island with drawers on each side; black and white marble floors and crown molding.

She admired the Mahagony armoire her grandmother had given her when she and Gavin purchased their first home. It was a family heirloom to remind her of her roots - the strength of the women who had come before her that allowed her to stand strong in the face of adversity.

Adriana slowly made her way to the left side of the closet. She stopped at the uniforms and the suits. She reached for Gavin's light-brown suit; he had worn it on his last business trip with Justus and Winston.

She carefully placed her hand into each of the inside pockets of his jacket. She pulled out a business card. "Blair Richardson, Realtor" was written on the back.

"Okay; he said they had met with a realtor about three properties they were thinking about purchasing," she said to herself.

She searched the outside pockets. Closed her eyes before turning the phone on. She was surprised it did not have a passcode. She looked at the phone's recent calls. They were all made to the same number.

"Do I really want to know?" Adriana asked herself out loud.

She recalled advice Grandma Ethel passed on that had been given to her by her grandmother, "All men have at least twenty-five percent dog in them. It just comes out in different ways and for different reasons."

Did she really want to know if Gavin was being a dog? Could she think of a reason Gavin would be a dog? She moved through a checklist in her mind. She could not find a reason.

Her palms began to sweat. She bit her lower lip then took a deep breath. If she did find what Cilicia said she would, what would she do?

She did not confide in her friends or mother about issues she had with Gavin. She felt that it took a man to help her understand a man, i.e., her confidence in her father and uncles.

The phone in Adriana's hand confirmed that Cilicia's revelations had some truth to them. She flipped the phone open again to study the number. It was not one she recognized, nor did it match the number on the business card.

Adriana searched her mind questioning where she went wrong. She thought about their time together prior to her pregnancy with Ariadne. Those early years of their marriage were well spent. Gavin transitioned from active duty in the Air Force to reserve and began working for one of the airlines. Ariadne was born during their third year of marriage, so it was solid by then. Nicklous arrived three years later when they understood parenthood and what needed to be done to make life work.

The years prior to Adriana's first pregnancy gave Gavin, Justus, and Winston time to save for their first real estate investment. The home she and Gavin had purchased in their first year of marriage became the second rental property for GJW Properties.

Grandma Ethel's words rang in Adriana's mind again. "Men love power and money. As women we have to find a way to balance the power between them and us. Money is one way to do that. This, my dear, is the advice my grandmother gave me, and she got it from her grandmother."

Adriana wished she could access her wisdom now. She looked down at the phone in her hand that was still open. Something inside of her wanted to call the number. Something inside of her did not want to betray the trust Gavin had in her.

"Gavin would never go through my clothes and phone," she reasoned.

She paused.

"Gavin would never let anything Justus or anyone else say about me cause him to question or marriage."

Her heart stopped.

She became numb and motionless.

She could not think.

She could not think.

She could not think.

Gavin was her world. Together they had built a life that she thought was only possible in books.

She carefully put things back the way she found them.

She crawled into her bed.

Her mind went blank for just a minute. Then it began to race. In the past, Gavin's time at work made her heart grow fonder. Now it was making her wonder exactly what he was doing when he was away.

The more her mind raced, the more she assumed a fetal position. She stayed that way until she heard a knock at the door.

"Adriana," Regenia called to her daughter. She made her way to her daughter's bed. "It's getting late. I thought we would've had dinner by now. What's wrong?"

Adriana sat up in her bed. "What would you like to eat, Mom. I will order in."

"What's wrong?"

"I'm just a little tired from the day."

"Did you get your papers graded?"

"Lunch with Cilicia was a bit long, so I didn't go to the park. There was a big difference in the wind here and the wind in the inner city, so I came home."

Adriana looked at her mom. She could tell by her quizzical expression that she was not convinced all was well.

"How about ordering Chinese tonight? We could get something healthy for you," Adriana suggested.

"Chinese is fine," Regenia agreed. "Are you getting up?"

"I'll be up in a few. Ask Ariadne to place the order for us. She likes doing that. Get a card out of my purse."

* * *

Adriana was awakened by the opening of her bedroom door. She rolled from her left side onto her right side. She rose slightly on her elbow ready to greet Nicklous, who usually came to wish her a good night if she was already in her room.

The shadowy figure was over a foot taller. As she adjusted her eyes to the height, she felt something swell inside of her.

Her heart began to flutter, and her root chakra began to react, to pulsate at the smell that was approaching her bed.

Gavin was taking off the jacket to his uniform as he bowed down to kiss the love of his life. Adriana perched her head to receive the kiss that always made things right in her world. She slid over a few inches to give him the space he always occupied to greet his queen when he returned home from work.

She looked into Gavin's eyes. It was still there - the look of love he always gave her. There was no doubt in her mind that she was still his queen; the center of his world.

But if this is true, then how could what Cilicia had shown her also be true.

"I thought you were meeting Gavin and Winston for the game." Adriana said to her husband.

"That was the plan. We needed an extra hand, so I accepted the flight to guarantee I would get homecoming weekend off."

"I wish you had called me. I didn't order food for you."

"I wanted to surprise you," Gavin said with a smile. "You gave me something better; your mother staying for a few days."

"Marissa has COVID and will be out for the next two weeks. Mama offered to stay until she feels better."

Adriana shrugged her shoulders.

"It's not like I could say, 'No;' she knows I need the help."

Gavin moved in closer to his wife. He leaned over and pushed her hair away from her forehead. He gently placed a kiss on it.

"I know how much you and the kids like having your mother around. It's okay, Adriana."

The sensation between Adriana's legs intensified. Gavin knew the look all too well. He unbuttoned his shirt. Adriana rubbed the hairs on his chest. He stood up then ripped his shirt off.

Adriana thought about what Cilicia had shown her. She watched Gavin as he continued to undress. Thoughts invaded her mind again.

Gavin leaned in closer to her with his naked body. The scent of his body erased all Cilicia had shown and told her. Gavin's hands touched her nipples. He cupped her breasts before he slipped her gown over her head.

Gavin's touch, his scent gave her arousal that melted as his lips touched hers.

There it was. The kiss that activated her root chakra twenty-one years ago. The kiss that made gave Gavin access to her sugar walls quicker than any other lover she had surrendered to in her past.

The tongue that moved in and out of her mouth made her give up all inhibitions. She opened herself to him, and he accepted the invitation. He moved inside of her with a rhythmic flow that triggered her seismic waves.

Twenty minutes later, Adriana released her hands from his back. She placed them above her head. Her earth was quaking.

Gavin knew what to do to increase the measurements on the Richter scale. By the sound of her release, it was a 6.9. Gavin moved a little more to the right – 7.9. He moved to the left - 8.9. Gavin released himself. He allowed his cream to mix with her honey without another move.

8

Borderlines

Cilicia rose from her knees with a heavy sigh. She had been taught her entire life to take her troubles to God in prayer.

"What goes on behind closed doors stays behind closed doors," is what her mother instructed her children to do.

Cilicia knew her mother was keeping secrets about their father to protect his reputation and their family in the community. There were times Cilicia had accidentally folded laundry and saw underwear that did not belong to her mother. She never let her mother know what she had seen.

"Some of those preachers who be stumping and shouting the loudest keep the most secrets," people used to say when she was in high school. That's why she chose not to return home after going off to college. She never attended any high school reunions because she didn't have any interest in seeing those people again.

She only made herself public during the annual Family and Friends Day at her father's church to please her parents and uphold their image. She protected herself from returning home by teaching

CONFUSION, COMPASSION, CONFESSION - 53

Sunday school in her own church and being busy in a few other organizations that did charitable work.

Talking to her mother about her suspicions and feelings about Justus's lifestyle was not an option for her. Adriana was upset with her when she tried to share her thoughts and feelings with her. She needed someone to talk to. She was alone and abandoned.

Cilicia was beginning to feel more desperate. Loneliness was growing in her heart. She wanted to feel Justus beside her and in her. She wanted to remember how it felt to have a husband to share her life with. The peaceful co-existence was not working, either; Justus didn't as much as acknowledge her presence most of the time.

She decided to try and get Justus's attention again. This time she chose the red, racerback chemise with G-string panties she bought on the after-Valentine's clearance rack. The lace daisies revealed her areolas, one part of her body Justus used to love to swirl his tongue around.

It was now 1:30 am, so Cilicia did not have to worry about Alexus and Evian; they should be asleep. She walked into the family room where Justus had made his sleeping area for the past two years.

As Cilicia made her way to the coach, she could see he was leaning over. She looked over his shoulder and saw the lines he had on a mirror, one of which he was consuming. She looked to his left and saw his tablet.

"Son-of-a-bitch! You bastard. You can't give your wife any attention because you spend your time snorting cocaine and watching gay porn. Or better yet, your ass is making gay porn. I hate you; you bastard! Get out!!!" Cilicia screamed in frustration and disappointment. She turned to leave.

Justus snapped his head in shock. He jumped across the couch and placed his hand around Cilicia's neck.

"You don't know what you're talking about!" he said, matching the force of his words with the power he had around her neck.

Cilicia tried to loosen his grip. She was struggling to breathe. She pushed his arm a little harder.

Justus pushed into her neck, tightening his grip. The look in Justus's eyes was of a fury she had never seen in him. Fearing for her life, Cilicia kicked him between his legs. He dropped his hand to cup himself. She rose from the floor then ran to the bedroom and locked the door.

Cilicia crawled into her bed. She felt as if she was in a bottomless pit. She had prayed to God for answers to heal her marriage, and this was what she got. There was nothing that could have prepared her for what had happened.

She knew that Justus had been smoking marijuana; she had seen the evidence years ago. She had seen painkillers around the house, too. He said that he needed them to help him with the injury he got playing football in high school. He had even blamed his pain and the medication for him not being able to perform like he used to.

But tonight told a different story. She saw his erected penis when he rose from the table; she saw him look at his tablet as he stroked it. There was no denying what she had seen.

Memories of her childhood flashed into her mind. She remembered one of her mother's brothers being upset at rumors of her father sleeping with another preacher from the community.

"They call him a pansy," her uncle said to her mother. "They even say he wears women's panties."

The image of her mother's face had been forever etched in Cilicia's memory – the look of confusion and shame. Cilicia recalled her own feelings when she realized the panties in her parents' laundry probably didn't belong to another woman but maybe her dad. Even with that, she knew her mother would never have a conversation with her about how to get through this.

She shook her head as the tears of loneliness fell from her eyes.

She felt sick. She went into her bathroom and sat by the toilet. She could feel the nausea, but nothing moved.

She thought about her mother – always poised and dignified. Nothing on her was ever out of place, not even a single hair.

Memories of her mother's arms being squeezed by her father as he pushed her into their bedroom crowded Cilicia's mind. She wasn't sure if that was the time her mother had suffered a broken arm; the time her mother told her children she had tripped over the chair in her bedroom, but Cilicia knew it was just to cover what she had heard her father do to her mother.

Cilicia turned pale as the blood left her face; she fell to the floor. She didn't have the strength to get up.

Finally, she staggered from the floor to her chair by the vanity. She pulled herself up. She checked her neck.

Alexus and Evian did not need to see what their father had done to her. As much as she hated him, she didn't want them to feel about their father the way she felt about hers.

She retrieved her make-up bags from the cabinet. She mixed foundations and powers until the bruises were hidden and her neck matched her face.

She put her bathrobe on. She left the room for the kitchen. Tears formed in her eyes when she saw Justus asleep on the coach. A part of her wanted to hurt him just like he had hurt her. She shook her head and walked away.

She went into the kitchen to make breakfast. Alexus and Evian were leaving at 6:00 for a band competition. She needed to have breakfast ready before they left. She went through the motions of cooking breakfast, trying her best not to alarm Justus.

She tiptoed to his office; the door was unlocked. She went to his desk drawer. She found a keyring that did not have his office and mailbox keys on it. She slipped the key into her robe. She found some documents that she had taken pictures of. His supply of cocaine and pills were in his desk, too. She checked the time then left.

* * *

The doorbell rang. Regenia was happy to see Cilicia. It had been a while since they had seen each other. Maybe she could get some answers from Cilicia to understand what had taken Adriana out of her usual self. Regenia always worried about Adriana when she was like this. The last time she was this way was after she had broken up with that "no good somethin' of another" she called him.

Regenia invited her to join her for coffee in the morning room. "I enjoy sitting in here before the kids get up," Regenia said.

She looked at Cilicia. "What has you up so early?"

"I had to get my kids off to band camp this morning," she answered.

"Where is Justus?"

"He's home."

"This would be a good time to sleep in with your husband," Regenia advised.

Cilicia looked at the floor. Regenia didn't say anything; she had all the answers she needed.

"He's a little tired right now. They have a client who is being audited by the IRS, so he has been putting in a lot of time with her."

"Oh; I understand," came the response from the woman who knew all too well how those things went.

"Sometimes, we must exert ourselves a little more. Our husbands get so lost in their work. They don't know when trouble is creeping up on them."

"Is that what happened to your marriage?" Cilicia asked, knowing that Regenia was more open to talking about her life than her own mother.

"He was doing a lot of work, but it wasn't always what was

benefiting our family. He got a little too much pleasure out of his work." Regenia sipped her coffee while looking in the distance.

"I'm feeling the same way about Justus."

Regenia lowered her coffee cup. She looked Cilicia in the eyes. She had no words for the younger version of herself. Marriages had always come with complications. The trick has always been determining which complications a person wanted to deal with.

Finally, Regenia spoke. "When was the last time the two of you spent time together without your children?"

"There doesn't seem to be enough time," Cilicia said.

"Do you ever go to the ball games with him?"

"I haven't been since Evian was a baby."

"That's one of the problems with our modern world. We have very little time for the important things," the elder woman said.

"It's not always my schedule," Cilicia stated.

Regenia looked over her glasses; she didn't need the extra lenses to see what was going on.

Adriana went into the morning room to join her mother. She was surprised and a bit put off when she saw Cilicia. She had neither seen nor spoken to her in over three weeks. She had purposely ignored her text messages and phone calls. She didn't want to hear anything she had to say about what Gavin MIGHT be doing.

She turned around to go back to her room. She paused. She did an about-face. She went into the morning room.

"Funny seeing you here," Adriana addressed Cilicia with a sharp look without greeting her mother.

"I invited her over," Regenia said to Adriana. "She called to talk to me, so I invited her over to have coffee with us."

That was just like Regenia. Never judging and trying to bring peace to every situation. Adriana's blood began to boil.

Adriana shifted her weight from her left side to the right. She lowered her hands from her hips then leaned against the wall. Maybe if she pressed them flat, she could resist the urge to punch the shit out of Cilicia.

"I made pumpkin spice coffee this morning." She announced to the friends. "I found it at that little coffee shop over in... What's that area called again?"

"Knowledge Park," Adriana reminded her.

"Yes; Knowledge Park."

Cilicia looked over at Adriana. "I'm sure it's a good blend," she said to Regenia.

Adriana pressed her back to the wall. "Did you and Justus get into a fight or something?"

The question shocked Cilicia. "Why would you ask that?"

"Did he choke you?" Adriana asked, noticing the heavy make-up on her neck.

Cilicia was flustered. Hiding bruises was something she had become accustomed to, so the questions were making her feel vulnerable.

"Look," Adriana said. "You know I've been avoiding you, so there must be a reason why you're here."

"I came to see your mom," Cilicia answered in a soft voice.

The anger had somewhat cooled in Adriana when she saw Cilicia's neck, but it was beginning to rise again. She didn't need to share her mother right now; she needed her more than she ever had before Cilicia brought this dilemma to her.

The toddler in her began to rise, too. She wanted to stomp out of the room. She struggled with the selfish feelings she was having. She wanted to tell Cilicia to go to her own parents; however, she knew that was not possible. She fought her anger as she fought back her tears.

She began to feel anger towards Cilicia's parents who lived in their own, religious, small-town world. She knew there was no way they could help her with something as complex as infidelity; however, she still felt a bit of disdain for them.

Adriana struggled with whether to go to her room to grade essays or stay and have breakfast with her mother and Cilicia. A part of her wanted to just give up and let Cilicia have her mother for the moment. But there was this other part of her saying, "She has taken enough from you already. Don't give in this time."

Adriana released one of the tears that had formed from her rage. She couldn't be safe anywhere. Cilicia had invaded her again.

Adriana decided to take the middle ground. She relaxed in the chaise lounge in the morning room, looking outside her window at the trees that began to announce to the world a change in the weather had come.

9

I Know I Love My Husband

Adriana took every advantage of her mother being at her house. She needed this time to finish grading the criticism papers. Students were anxious about the grade they earned because the essay was twenty percent of their grade for the quarter. She decided to take advantage of the October warmth, so she went back to Romare Bearden to get some sunlight to inspire her to finish the task.

> *I understand how the author could want to end her life if she didn't feel loved by her husband. I felt like that when my boyfriend wanted us to take a break from each other this year. I thought we would get married after we finished college. We had planned to go to the same school until he got offers to run cross-country. He said he wanted to attend one of those schools he got the offers from instead of Carolina with me. He said that we could get back together after college after we had explored other options.*
>
> *Now I feel a little lost, so I can understand how the author might have felt lost. I don't think the author was a bad person for attempting*

suicide. People think about suicide all the time; they might not do everything to make it happen.

Sometimes people might be trying to get attention. This could be what the author was doing when she mentioned the two times she tried to commit suicide. The times I took pills I really didn't want to die. I just wanted someone to understand that I was really hurting because the plans I had made were not going to happen. If people do not feel like they have someone who hears them or even care, they might think about leaving this place.

Grading this paper made Adriana think about Cilicia. She was almost sure those were bruises on her neck that she tried to cover with make-up. A part of her felt happy that her mother was there to listen to her friend; however, there was another part of her that wished she didn't have to give up the opportunity to share with her mother what she was going through.

The pictures Cilicia had shown Adriana never left her mind. She thought about them incessantly. It was bad enough that she sometimes imagined him making love to the girlfriends he admitted to having before her while they had sex. Now she had to ask herself if that was really Gavin's penis Blair had in her mouth. She had refused to look at the picture long enough to examine the penis to see if it belonged to her husband; she didn't have to study it to know it was Blair.

Blair often talked about her husband's sexual inexperience and how she needed periodic maintenance to keep her marriage together. She never shared names with Adriana, but she would share experiences.

"He's not into anal," Blair once said, "so I let my maintenance man take care of that. His wife isn't into anal, so it's a win-win for us both."

The pit of Adriana's stomach fell. She gagged. Was she the woman Blair was talking about? Adriana's blood began to boil again.

She had never used the gifts God gave her even though she knew she had them. She was damn sure beginning to think about using them now – one pain deserved another. She thought again about a conversation she had with Blair about her anal sex lover.

She squinted her eyes. If she played that game, she knew she would slay more than a dragon. She sat in her anger. Then she gagged.

Adriana had not noticed the sun that was beaming down on her was now being blocked.

"Sorry I didn't bring a barf bag with me," a familiar voice said to her.

Adriana looked up.

"Athra," she said with a bit of surprise and relief. She pushed the papers and laptop aside and quickly jumped to her feet.

Athra, who was just as surprised and thrilled to see Adriana, opened her arms to receive and give the hug she knew was about to come.

"How have you been?" Athra asked. "How are the kids and Gavin? Your mom?"

Adriana assured her everyone was doing fine.

"That's good to hear."

"Where are you headed?" Adriana asked.

"I was just taking a few minutes to enjoy this beautiful October weather before heading to the Gnatt museum."

Athra briefly studied Adriana's face. She could sense that Adriana needed something. "I think I will sit over there for a few minutes. How about joining me?"

Adriana gathered her laptop and papers then placed them in her backpack.

"Why are you working so hard on a sunny, Saturday afternoon?"

"I am grading criticism papers. My students' thoughts on 'Lady Lazarus' and Sylvia Plath are interesting. It's time to take a break after the last one I just read."

"Men - can't live without them." Athra commented. "Dying in each decade; I can see how that happens. Death doesn't have to mean our physical bodies. It could mean death of ideas, ways of living, ways of being."

Athra looked in the direction of the stadium then at her friend. She was several years older than Adriana - six to be exact. They had met when Athra was working a part-time job to supplement her income and Adriana was going into her senior year of high school. That summer had forged a friendship that had endured for almost thirty years.

The ladies reached the bench and sat down.

"Have your thoughts and ideas about things changed a lot since you became a minister?" Adriana asked her friend.

"I can't say they have changed much. I think I see things more universally than I did before turning forty, or maybe I just accept things more without judgment."

"Is that what being a minister is about to you?"

"I'm still in the love and healing business; that's what ministry is about for me."

"Have you ever questioned if God might judge you for your divorce?"

Athra lowered her hand from her forehead. "You're not thinking of divorce, are you?"

"Asking for a friend."

Athra turned her head and looked at Adriana over her glasses.

"It really is for a friend. If it was me, I would let you know."

Athra looked at her phone. "Is your number still the same?"

"I haven't changed it since I married Gavin."

"Check your phone. I sent you a message. Give me a call; we can continue this conversation then."

Something in Adriana's voice disturbed Athra; she felt she wouldn't have the time to focus on what her friend really needed. She knew Adriana enough to know that when those questions came, she would need time to sort things out.

"I am a part of the panel discussion today. Give me a call next week; I will make time for you."

Adriana knew she could trust those words.

The two rose in unison. They departed with hugs, and Adriana returned to grading papers. Monica's paper was next.

> Women have been forced to give up their dreams and live in the shadow of men their whole lives. Some of the most brilliant women have suppressed who they truly are because society would not accept women in certain positions or doing certain things. Sylvia knew she was very talented and believed in herself. That is why she wrote that she would rise from the ashes of her heartbreaks and disappointments to be great and do great things.
>
> A part of me wants to condemn her for attempting suicide a third time. She was delusional to think she could try it again and rise like Lazarus. Thinking that she had nine lives like a cat was proof that she had a serious mental illness. If she could've focused more on her writing instead of her marriage or disappointments she had experienced in life, maybe she would've met God and Lucifer after she had become the writer she knew she would be at a much later time.

Adriana was relieved all the essays were graded and entered in the gradebook. She was happy to be able to close the chapter on the first quarter of the school year.

In the Middle of the Night

Dear Diary,

I can't sleep. It is 4:00 in the morning, and I should be asleep. But I can't because I realize that I have been so caught up in wanting to love someone and wanting to be loved. All my energy has been focused on doing that. I have always placed Gavin's needs before my own without realizing what I was doing. Between reading my students' essays and Cilicia being in my face, I am beginning to question things about my life.

This weekend away from Gavin and the children is giving me the opportunity to really look within. Last night was so difficult for me. This was the first time I had been without Gavin and the children at the same time.

Gavin, Winston, and Justus went to their homecoming weekend. This silence has Cilicia's voice in my head and questioning everything I believe about my marriage. What if what Cilicia has been saying about our husbands is true? What if she has been telling Sheraton the same things about Winston that she has been telling me about Gavin?

I am excited to have the time alone because I need a break. But all I can think about is Gavin being intimate with someone else. Gavin and his friends have always gone to college football games, but it has never bothered me until now.

My mind wouldn't let me sleep because I am thinking about all the things that Gavin could've done last night and with whom. I don't know if I would be feeling this way if I thought Gavin was having sex with someone I don't know.

The first picture Cilicia showed me has me questioning if Gavin is…. I don't know if I would be feeling so confused and uncertain if I could find evidence Gavin is having an affair with a woman. I know that I am feeling trapped within myself and imprisoned in this marriage. Who do you talk to about your feelings when you suspect our husband is having an unconventional affair?

I've read some blogs about people having different lifestyles. In one situation fraternity brothers plan weekend get-a-ways with each other during football season. Most of the brothers are married, and their wives never seem to suspect that they are lovers.

In another blog a wife was suspicious of her husband having an affair. She confided in her husband's best friend who is his frat brother and the one he is getting it on with.

Another wife suspected her husband was having sex with a man when she discovered pictures in the trunk of his car. That wife decided to limit the amount of sex she had with her husband, which is how she justified all the one-night-stands she has with other men. She didn't feel like she could talk to anyone about her discovery, so sex became her therapy.

In some ways I feel like that character. Who can I talk to about my thoughts and feelings right now? My mom? Courtney? My dad? My gay cousin? My bisexual uncle? There is no one I can talk to about this. So, I just keep my thoughts to myself and try to act as if nothing is wrong.

But who am I kidding? How long can I last like this? How long can I pretend that I am okay every time Gavin is on the phone with one of his friends? How long can I keep pretending that it does not bother me when he is out with his boys? I don't even trust him when he goes to work. I wonder what he does during his layovers and if he is really working all the time he says he is.

I have been watching a show about people with sex addictions. One of the men who was seeing the therapist had a problem with having sex with men. He would spontaneously meet men on the way to work and have sex with them without even knowing their names. He didn't understand why he had the urge to do something like that. He even admitted that he was happily married and had a great sex life with his wife.

All of this is messing with my head. I have a lump in my throat. Tears are wailing up in my eyes; I am doing my best to keep them from falling. I don't think I love my husband. I know I love my husband. I know I want to keep my family together, but I don't know how without losing myself.

I WANT MY LIFE BACK! I WANT MY HUSBAND BACK! I WANT TO KNOW THAT I AM THE MOST IMPORTANT THING IN HIS LIFE! I WANT HIM TO HOLD ME AND MAKE LOVE TO ME AND CARESS MY FACE! I WANT TO KNOW THAT WE HAVE A BOND THAT IS SO TIGHT NOTHING COULD EVER THREATENED IT! I WANT TO BE THE LOVE OF HIS LIFE!

Gavin was supposed to be the answer to my prayers. He was supposed to protect me from ever feeling this way. I am going crazy here. I don't know what to do anymore. I feel so lost and all alone.

Oh, God! Please, HELP ME!

10

He Loves His Wife

The sound of the alarm being disarmed was what woke Adriana from her sleep. She wasn't expecting her mother and the children until dinner time. Before she could get out of bed, Gavin appeared in the doorway; she wasn't expecting him until around lunchtime.

"You're early," she said to her husband.

"I decided to leave when I woke up. I want to spend some time with you before the kids get home."

A part of Adriana felt excited while another part of her felt as if she needed more time. A part of her felt gratitude for him wanting to spend time with her while another part of her felt frustration because it was hard for her to feel anything but love for him when he was in her presence.

Gavin looked into his wife's eyes. Any anger she wanted to hold on to flushed from her body. Without a thought, she slid over to make room for him. He sat on the edge and held her by her shoulders.

"I love, Adriana."

"I love you, too, Gavin."

He began to unbutton her pajama top to expose her breasts. He used both hands to cup them. Her right hand glided to his torso. She lifted his shirt then played with his navel. He leaned over and kissed her. His tongue glided into her mouth, and he teased her with an in and out motion. She knew exactly what was in store for her; her root chakra confirmed it for her.

Adriana couldn't get the pictures Cilicia had shown her out of her mind. She looked over at the fruit Gavin sat on the nightstand then she looked at her husband. Visions of the picture of Blair with the penis in her mouth danced in her head. She pushed Gavin on his back.

She took one of the strawberries and split it open. She rubbed it up and down the shaft of his penis. Gavin looked at his wife in total surprise. She placed the strawberry on the head of his penis then grabbed her phone and took a picture of it.

Gavin's nostrils flared. Adrianna placed her mouth over the strawberry and pleased her husband in a way she had never done before. Gavin surrendered himself to the moment.

Adriana crawled on top of him.

The foreplay had Adriana more than ready for Gavin. Her vagina wrapped around this penis; in less than two minutes she experienced her first orgasm. With each thrust of his penis, Adriana's sugar walls responded with a massage that gave him just enough room to move the way he wanted to. Their bodies smelted into one, maintaining the vows they made seventeen years ago.

Adriana knew she had to fight for her marriage one way or another. She didn't want to discuss with Gavin the things Cilicia had said and shown to her. All she knew was that she wanted her husband.

"Oh, Gavin," she whispered in his ear. "I don't know what I would do if you ever made anyone else feel the way you make me feel."

Gavin turned her onto her stomach.

"You never have to worry about that," he promised.

He lifted her to her knees then carried her to the place he knew she loved to go. Then he released himself in her.

Reaching her ultimate climax always made Adriana feel vulnerable yet free. Gavin had the ability to do things to her body that she never knew it could do. She snuggled in her husband's arms. Being there with him reminded her of what he had given her – the type of love she thought only existed in fairytales, security and freedom to be herself, and two children whom she loved so much.

* * *

Adriana went into the kitchen. She was happy to see coffee had been brewed. She made herself a cup. Gavin had blended the Kenyan and Costa Rican coffees to get a new flavor. Adriana admired how her husband liked to try new things.

For a moment, her mind went to Cilicia and their conversations. As she sipped on her coffee, she was reminded of how much Gavin did to show his love for her. She tried so hard to reconcile the man she had left in bed with the man Cilicia was trying to make her believe her husband was.

She said to herself, "I love Gavin; I cannot deny that. He has given me my happily ever after. When he is not at home, my arms miss him. He has taken away all the insecurities I felt about love; he has made me a believer, or am I lying to myself?"

Cilicia had done something to her that she never thought would happen. How could she reconcile her reality with the threat that was constantly being pushed in her face. For months now, Cilicia was being relentless in her efforts to make Adriana look at what was bothering her.

Adriana sipped her coffee; she loved the way the flavors blended. It was these things that she loved about her husband; his thoughtfulness – the way he cared for her were all signs that he loved and appreciated his marriage.

"I thought you were coming down to make breakfast," Gavin's voice echoed in the kitchen as he reached the last two stairs.

The sound startled Adriana. She thought she would be alone; she needed the space to think things through.

"I am making breakfast. We're having shrimp and grits." She pointed to the simmering gravy.

She wanted to do whatever she could to fight for her marriage. Or, in the alternative, never give Gavin a clue that she was suspicious of his affair.

Lady Lazarus

I am at it again;
Life is leaving me.

I have nothing to hold on to;
I have nothing to BELIEVE in;
Everything I had HOPED for;
Everything I had WISHED for;
Everything I had WORKED for;
The **DREAM** is gone from me.

11

Feeling Vulnerable

Adriana walked into the robin's egg blue office taking a deep breath. She immediately felt the calm she had needed since her last conversation with Cilicia.

She regretted even answering her phone call. There was nothing she, Adriana, could do to fix what had been broken for over ten years. Plus, she was in her own predicament now.

Athra rose from her chair to greet Adriana.

Adriana took notice of her friend. She admired the sleeveless, wide legged, turquoise jumpsuit. To her surprise, curiosity rose in her. She wasn't sure exactly what it was. Could it be that she was meeting Athra in an office instead of a restaurant or one of their homes? Or was something else happening?

"Where would you like to sit today?" the spiritual therapist asked.

"I need the lounge today," Adriana answered leading the way to that area of the office space.

Athra followed then took a seat in her tulip chair made in a gray jacquard with light gold leaves.

Adriana took a seat in the chaise lounge that matched the armchair her therapist was sitting in. Within a few seconds she rose from her seat. She reached into her bag and pulled out the throw she had packed. She unfolded the throw then carefully stretched it onto the lounge. Returning to a sitting position, she kicked the three-inch pumps off her feet. They landed on the floor with a thump. She sprawled her body across the lounge chair.

Athra's eyebrows rose. She had seen that Adriana before – before she started dating Gavin. So, the return to this Adriana was beginning to make her worry.

"Comfortable?" Athra asked, with a little smile on her face.

Adriana, laying on her back with her right leg relaxing on the lounge chair and her left leg dangling from the side rested her right elbow on the lounge as she placed her hand on her forehead. She took two deep breaths before the tears began to fall.

Athra continued her observation of Adriana. She took a note. A couple of minutes passed as the two sat in silence.

"I feel vulnerable," Adriana confessed. "I feel vulnerable," she reiterated.

A crease formed between Athra's eyebrows.

"Why do you feel vulnerable?" she asked for clarity.

"Gavin has always been my haven. Now I feel that space has been penetrated," Adriana revealed.

Athra shifted her weight to her left hip then crossed her legs. "Your statement intrigues me," she stated.

Adriana slid her right leg off the lounge chair as she sat on the edge of her seat. She dabbed her eyes with the tissue she had retrieved from her bag when she took out her throw.

"I have never discussed my martial problems with anyone,"

Adriana disclosed. "My own mother has no idea what I am dealing with in my marriage."

She pursed her lips together before biting her lower lip. She wanted to say the words but wasn't sure how she would appear to her friend. Athra had always been open-minded and accepting, so she wasn't sure if she was projecting her own thoughts and feelings.

Adriana looked up at Athra who seemed to be barely breathing as if she was bracing herself for some bad news. Adriana could read the anticipation on her face.

"She's a minister," Adriana thought to herself. "There is nothing you can say to her that she has not heard."

Adriana closed her eyes. She could feel the tears roll just as they had seventeen years ago. She admitted to herself that she loved Gavin more than anyone else she had ever loved in her life. She could not think about her children without thinking about their father. She could not think about herself without Gavin being a part of her life.

Adriana looked at Athra's perfect persona. She saw a woman who seemed to have everything figured out in life; she always had. Adriana admired how Athra always had herself well put together. Her clothes seemed tailor-made to fit her figure. Her makeup had such a natural look that it did not mask her true beauty. Athra's earrings and necklaces always drew people into her eyes. Eyes that drew people into her.

Adriana bit her upper lip. Again, she looked up at Athra. She shifted in her seat. She wanted to speak but the lump in her throat would not allow her to. She lowered her gaze.

She began to question why she could not say the words that would set her free. She wanted to be free – freedom was something she had wanted since her childhood. Freedom to express herself – that thing that was guaranteed by the Constitution of the United States but suppressed by proper manners and etiquette.

The image of her conversation with Cilicia permeated her thoughts. She began to privately acknowledge that her feelings for Cilicia had changed. The person she felt was her best friend had become her enemy.

Adriana looked up. She could only imagine what Athra was hiding behind her own persona. She recalled a conversation they had a few years ago.

"Most therapists and preachers are on a path of healing themselves. Some of us for what has happened to us, and some of us for what we have done to others. A few of us are on a journey because of both."

Adriana wondered which one was Athra and if she would be opening her closet. She always wondered what led to Athra's divorce. She never talked about the details, so it kept Adriana wondering what had happened to what seemed like the perfect marriage.

Without thinking, Adriana divulged, "I feel vulnerable because Cilicia has penetrated my safe space."

"Continue," Athra encouraged.

"Cilicia visited me last week. She was upset because our husbands have been swinging," Adriana continued.

"The conversation made you feel vulnerable?" Athra asked again.

"Yes," Adriana softly answered. "If Cilicia knows our husbands have been swinging, then how many other people know?"

"Is that a question you need an answer to?"

"My marriage has been the one thing I could count on that was the way I wanted it to be," Adriana acknowledged. "It was everything I always dreamed of and wanted. Gavin has always treated me the way I wished my father had treated my mother."

"Has any of that changed?" Athra questioned.

"What do you mean? Everything has changed. How can I live a life where people know my husband is unfaithful to me?" Adriana wanted to know.

"My question to you, Adriana, is this. Has Gavin changed towards you?"

"No. He doesn't even know I know."

"Why do you feel vulnerable?"

Adriana looked towards the window. "I feel vulnerable because my life has changed."

"How has your life changed?"

"My life has changed by Cilicia confronting me about our husbands' swinging. My life has changed because I have found two phones that my husband has been hiding from me. My life has changed because once a woman finds these things out about her husband, it is time for her to leave," Adriana asserted.

"Are you sure?" Athra asked.

"Sure, about what?" Adriana presented.

"Are you sure that your life has to change, AND are you sure it is time for you to leave?" were the interrogating questions Athra presented to Adriana for an analysis and clear answer.

"When things like this happen, people leave their marriages. Marriage is supposed to be sacred. Having affairs is not a part of the agreement."

"Is this why you are feeling vulnerable?"

"I feel vulnerable because Cilicia knows what Gavin has been doing. She said that she will not stay with Justus. She plans to get a divorce. I almost feel like I need to get one, too," Adriana declared.

"Cilicia's life is not your life," Athra said.

"Cilicia knows what Gavin has been doing. She said our husbands have been swinging," Adriana argued.

"What exactly did Cilicia say to you?" Athra asked.

"She told me that our husbands have been swinging with members of an accounting group," Adriana informed.

"Okay," Athra said.

"Cilicia said that she found a phone Justus uses to arrange sex parties. She read text messages that gave dates and times." Adriana shook her head; tears flowed from her eyes. "I feel like I have been living in a bubble." She sucked her teeth. "I didn't know that a gnome in a person's front yard is code to indicate the homeowners are swingers." Adriana said.

She wiped her nose then looked up at Athra. "You learn something every day."

"Okay," Athra said. "That still does not explain why you think you must end your marriage."

"Cilicia told me that she recognized one of my friend's numbers in the phone. She looked back at some group texts I've sent and found a church member's cell phone number. She told me that my friend Blair from church is one of the people in the group. Neither she nor her husband is an accountant."

Adriana looked down at her feet. "And she wouldn't stop until she found the proof she needed to throw in my face."

"Proof of what?"

"Cilicia showed me a picture of Blair giving someone a blow job. She told me it was Gavin. I refused to look at the picture to see if the penis belonged to Gavin; I just didn't want to add fuel to the fire that was burning in her and igniting in me. I didn't want to become a part of whatever she had going on."

"Is that what's bothering you?" Athra asked.

"Yes; I feel vulnerable to Blair, too. I feel like she has been a part of something very sacred to me," Adriana said with tears in her voice.

"Cilicia never liked her," she continued. "She always said that Blair was a whore. Cilicia warned me about allowing her to be a part of my life and letting her come into my home," Adriana disclosed. "I gave her the benefit of the doubt because we were both married, Christian women with children close in age to each other. She was someone who I really enjoyed a friendship with."

"You are talking about something else now," Athra stated.

"No; it is all the same. I am dealing with the fact that I found a phone in Gavin's jacket pocket. There are pictures of a woman giving a blowjob. The man is only visible from his waist down to his mid-thighs. The woman is wearing a wig, so I don't know if it is Blair or some other person," Adriana analyzed.

"I cannot deny that the first picture she showed me was a picture of Blair. I neither confirmed nor denied it was Gavin. I was so upset with her for betraying a promise we made to each other; I couldn't bring myself to inspect the picture to see if it was Gavin's penis," she admitted.

"Knowing that Gavin has been swinging with Blair makes me feel like more than just Cilicia knows that my marriage has been a lie," Adriana admitted.

"Adriana, has Gavin changed towards you?" Athra asked.

"You are not listening to me," Adriana said, increasing the volume of her voice with a certain firmness. "My husband has been having sex with other women. People I am close to know about it. One of the people who I thought was my friend is one of those women."

"Okay. What needs to happen now?" Athra asked.

"I don't know what needs to happen now," Adriana admitted shaking her head. She sat silently in her emotions.

She looked at the aquarium and noticed how the catfish moved in the water among the other fish. It seemed to stick to the bottom of the aquarium hiding within the wood. It didn't swim to the upper level like some of the more colorful and fast-moving fish.

"Gavin works so hard to craft the perfect life. He kisses me when he leaves home and when he comes back. He acknowledges every anniversary, birthday, Mother's Day, Valentine's Day, and Christmas with wonderful gifts. He knows how much I love jewelry, so he surprises me with something beautiful each year. He holds me close when he comes to bed at night. He takes time to help me deal with whatever problem I am facing. Gavin spends time with the children and attends almost every event they are involved in. I never have to worry about money, or anything not being taken care of. He has worked our entire marriage to give me whatever I have asked for," Adriana said as the catfish caught her attention again.

She shook her head. "Gavin has been operating his life like a smooth criminal," she said under her breath.

"Adriana, you just listed all the things you love about your husband," Athra said taking her out of her daze.

"How do I stay married to a man who is living a double life?" Adriana asked.

"Is he living a double life?"

"I feel as if he is."

Athra looked at her watch.

"Listen, I have an appointment that just arrived," Athra announced. "We can continue our conversation in an hour, or you can schedule an appointment to come in next week."

Adriana held her breath for a few moments as she contemplated her options. She wanted to stay and talk but needed more time to process what Cilicia had disclosed to her and what she had found.

"I will schedule an appointment for next week," Adriana answered.

"Between now and then, make a list of the things you love about Gavin and all the things that make your marriage a good one. Also think about the things you don't like about him and the things that are challenges in your marriage."

Athra made her way to Adriana and embraced her.

"We'll get through this together, Adriana. We always have."

"Thanks, Athra. You never had to help me get through a marriage."

"True; there's always a first time for everything. See you next week," then Athra led the way to the door.

Dear Diary,

I had a session with Athra today. I couldn't bring myself to say what Cilicia told me she really believes about our husbands. How can I tell her that Cilicia said she saw naked pictures of Gavin on Justus's phone? How can I tell her that Cilicia feels like our husbands have been in a bromance for years.

Cilicia told me about a time when we went on a couple's trip. She said she found blood in Justus's underwear. She said that she questioned him about it; he said that it was hemorrhoids. She said that something inside of her never believed it was hemorrhoids. She said that she never questioned him any more about it; however, she could never forget it.

She said she has been feeling more confused about her marriage. She is not the only one.

I am feeling so confused at this point, too.

P.S. I HATE HER FOR WHAT SHE HAD DONE TO ME!

12

Fight For Your Husband, Chile

Cilicia was nestled on her sofa. The holiday scene from the series she was watching caught her attention. The couple was making love by the fireplace close to the Christmas tree. They were enjoying each other's presence more than the presents they had received. She thought about the first few Christmases she had with Justus and the times they made love on the living room floor. She reminisced about the days she could enjoy a football game or romantic movie with Justus. She even missed the days she would watch a movie with Alexus and Evian. Memories of her own childhood danced through her head.

Thanksgiving dinner at her grandparent's house was so much fun. She looked forward to pulling the name of one of her dozens of cousins for Christmas. She thought about the first time she brought Justus home for Thanksgiving. Her grandfather had said to her,

"He ain't too bright, so he'll be a hard worker." She giggled at the memory.

Her grandfather was right about Justus being a hard worker. He spent most of his time in his office when he came home from work. He would eat dinner with his wife and children, but then he would rush back to his office.

So many things about that were confusing Cilicia. Their bank accounts did not reflect all the work Justus appeared to be doing. Despite all the work he said he was doing and the adjunct position she had taken, the numbers were going down instead of up.

She thought about the night she had seen him on the couch. So much was going through her head.

"Pray for your husband," is the advice she had always been given from her mother and aunties. "Always pray, chile, things always get better."

"I don't want things to get better when the best of us is gone," Cilicia thought to herself. "I want things to get better while we're still young."

Cilicia rose from the coach. She went into her bedroom and changed the sheets to the emerald green she used for special occasions. It had been years since those sheets had been on their bed - almost eight to be exact. They were last used in celebrating their dating anniversary.

Cilicia smiled at the happy memory but quickly became sadden. Eight years ago, that was when she began making appointments with her husband to have sex with her. Foreplay had become a thing of the past; sex had become more of a duty or obligation for him, or at least that is how it felt to Cilicia. Eventually, that stopped working, too.

She desired and needed to be touched by her husband; she needed him to validate her. She needed to feel his penis inside of her to let her know she was still important to him. Even though sex had become methodical to him, at least they were having it.

She continued to search her mind as to how she could fight for her husband – her husband and their family.

"The devil is a lie," she said aloud. "I will not allow MY husband and household to be overtaken by the enemy! God, I claim it in your name and the name of Jesus!"

She went into the bathroom and stood in front of the full-length mirror. She inspected her body, taking notice of the things that had changed since her wedding day. Weight – 20 extra pounds, a few stretch marks – on her thighs and breast, and hemangiomas that began appearing on her torso after giving birth to Alexus didn't make her body unattractive.

She drew a bath then slid in the bubbles to perfume her body. Every inch of her body was carefully attended to with the mittens she had placed on her hands. She pulled out her razor. Areas of her body that were beginning to show stubble were given extra attention.

Cilicia got out of her bath and walked to the shower to rinse off. She gently patted dry then massaged moisturizer in her skin to make it feel silky smooth. She sprayed perfume behind each ear, near her sacral chakra, behind her knees, and on each inner thigh. Justus loved fragrances; he drenched himself in fragrances before leaving home.

She searched her wardrobe for the perfect ensemble. She found it – the cranberry and lace bra and crotchless panty set with the matching satin and lace chemise. She found her four-inch, cranberry, platform stilettos she wore to last year's Christmas party. Finally, she finished her look with the Brazilian, wavy wig that extended just above her hip bone. She checked herself in the mirror. This used to be one of Justus's favorite role-playing looks.

Cilicia walked down the stairs and looked for her husband on the couch; he wasn't there. A part of her felt relief; at least he wasn't doing what she had seen him do the last time he was on the couch. She went to his office; no Justus.

"Where could he be?" she questioned aloud.

Just as she was about to return upstairs, she heard the garage door open. She looked at the clock; it was past 2:00 am.

"Why would the garage door be opening?" she thought.

Fear began to arise in her. She took her shoes off and held them in her hand. She thought about the lines that were on the coffee table; she felt confusion and fear. She leaned on the kitchen counter.

Justus entered the kitchen from the laundry room. He was surprised to see Cilicia. She looked up at him. She turned her back to him and remained silent. She didn't quite know how to handle the situation.

Cilicia replaced the shoes she had taken off; she rose from the barstool she had sat on. She looked at Justus with determination.

"How long has this been going on?" She had found her voice.

Justus rubbed his nose. He walked to her and looked down into her eyes. Something about her look and the determination in her eyes caused him to get aroused. He untied the robe that had hidden the ruby he knew was inside. He slipped his hand inside.

Cilicia pushed his hand away.

"I'm your husband; you don't push my hand away!"

Cilicia turned to walk away. She had seen that look before and didn't want to tackle it.

Justus quickly took a sidestep to block her from leaving. Cilicia could see the devil was in him. Memories of the last time he was like this created more fear in her.

Justus looked at her then put one hand inside of her and the other around her neck. He turned her around then pushed her against the counter. Tears began to swell in Cilicia's eyes. He held her face to the counter and did more damage to the already fragile woman he had promised to love, honor, and protect. When he finished taking his anger out on her, he lifted his hand from her face.

"You want to know how long this has been going on? Longer than you can imagine, and it won't stop."

Cilicia struggled to walk up the stairs. To her surprise, Alexus was standing at the top of the stairs with tears streaming down her face.

"Mama," the teenager whispered, "you don't have to take that from Daddy."

Cilicia felt too ashamed to look at her daughter, so she walked past her as if she had not heard her speak.

* * *

Cilicia awoke from her sleep with pain, pain she had never felt. She struggled to get out of bed. She scooted to Justus's nightstand where he kept a secret stash of painkillers. She took one then fell asleep.

Cilicia was awakened by the knock at her door.

"Mama, me and Evian are leaving now," Alexus informed her mother.

Too ashamed to face her, Alexus instructed her to enter but kept her back to her.

"Mama, our ride is here. We are leaving for the competition."

"Okay," Cilicia responded in a raspy voice.

"Are you okay, Mama?"

"Yes; I'm fine. Have a good time. Text me when you get there."

"To school?"

"To the competition."

"I love you, Mama."

"I love you, too," Cilicia responded still not facing her daughter.

Alexus left the room without another word. This was not the first time she had seen her mother like this; it was just the worst time.

* * *

"Hello," Cilicia answered her phone with a raspy voice, working hard to calibrate herself to her surroundings.

"I'm sorry for awakening you," the voice on the other end of the phone said.

Cilicia eased herself to a sitting position; she cleared her throat. "Sheraton."

"I was calling to make sure we're still on for today; remember?"

"Oh, yeah," Cilicia cleared her throat. She looked at the clock on her nightstand. It was after eleven. "What time did we plan to meet?"

"We had talked about a lunch meeting; one o'clock?"

"One o'clock it is. Where?"

"We were meeting the caterer and decorator at Dynasty's; remember?" Cilicia reminded.

"Okay; I will meet you there."

Cilicia pushed the red button on her phone. She reached into Justus's nightstand again then fell asleep.

13

The Kiss of Death

Adriana drove down the boulevard in the middle lane. She often did that because it was easier to switch lanes in case of an emergency. The urgency in Sheraton's voice and the fact that Cilicia was not answering her phone motivated her to leave the Sanctuary. The past few months had put so much toxicity into Adriana's life, she was trying her best to find her way back to the tranquil place that allowed her to believe that everything she had prayed for was what she was experiencing.

Usually, Adriana would be zipping by other motorists going at least five miles above the speed limit, but today she was different. She was contemplating how she would handle whatever situation Cilicia might be in or had created. All she knew was that Sheraton's voice was in a state of panic.

Cilicia's accusations had brought back a time from her past that she thought was behind her - a time when she had contemplated and even attempted suicide. She was beginning to hate Cilicia even more. The longer this went on, the more time she spent in her past.

Those memories bombarded her as she drove to Cilicia's home. Adriana thought about the baby she had forgotten and why.

* * *

It was twenty-two years ago when she had just finished her last day of internship at the Museum of Natural History. The after-work celebration ended quite early, so Adriana went to the apartment she shared with other interns and packed her bags. She called the girl she shared her bedroom with to let her know she was headed home early.

Adriana made the four and half hours trip back to Greensboro where she would begin her senior year at North Carolina A & T University in less than a month. She wanted to surprise the man she knew would someday become her husband. She recalled how happy she felt driving I-95 and how she dreamed of the wedding she would have to wed Jamie.

She put Mariah Carey's "When I Saw You" on repeat. Each time she reached a certain lyric, she thought about the first time she saw Jamie's eyes and what his eyes said back to her. She sang along as best she could. She had planned to have that song as their first dance. Jamie told her that he knew he wanted her to be in his life forever the first time he saw her walk into his frat house. It took about a month of secretly pursuing her before he gave in to his request for a date. He was one of the guys many girls had dated and even more wanted to date.

As she arrived in the parking lot of his apartment building, she noticed his car was not there. She used the key he had given her to let herself in. She was happy he wasn't there because she wanted to take a shower and surprise him when he got to his bedroom.

She carried her overnight bag upstairs. As she opened the door, she saw Jamie in another man's embrace. She stood paralyzed at the sight. He was kissing the man who was caressing his arched back.

She gasped as Jamie rolled his hips then turned his head to her. The man withdrew his erect penis from Jamie.

"What the fuck, Adriana," Jamie shouted. "What the hell are you doing here?"

Adriana could not move. She stood in a daze as Jamie jumped out of the bed. His erect penis instantly went limp. A man she did not know slid off the bed and reached for his clothes that were lying on the floor. He got dressed then left without saying a word.

Adriana looked at Jamie with disbelief as he put his pants on.

"What are you doing here?" Jamie asked again with anger.

Adriana looked him in his eyes with tears streaming from hers.

"I came home early to surprise you," she answered with a firmness in her voice that astonished even her.

Jamie looked at her with a sternness she had never seen before. He extended his left arm then grabbed her with a quickness.

Reflexes made her reach for the hand that had tightened around her neck. She tried to push him away, but he didn't move. He stared at her with a fire in his eyes that made her think she was being confronted by the devil himself. She kept trying to pry his hand from around her neck.

"Bitch," she heard him say. "You should've stayed your ass in Washington and came home when you were supposed to!"

The grip tightened. She kicked him between his legs; that made him loosen his grip. She turned towards the door. He yanked her ponytail, moved in front of her, then punched her in her face. She fell to the floor. He stood over her and was about to punch her again.

"JAMIE! NO!" she cried out. "WHAT'S WRONG WITH YOU!" she yelled as she scurried away from him.

"GET THE FUCK OUTTA HERE!" he demanded of her.

Adriana hurried down the stairs and into her car. She went to a hotel, called Courtney, and told her what happened. Just as cousins always do, Courtney came to her rescue. She spent the night with Adriana before carrying her home with her.

Adriana thought about the positive pregnancy test she had taken before leaving Washington. After everything that happened, she could not have a baby with Jamie. She cut her stomach and her wrist. The wounds were deep enough to put her in the hospital but not deep enough to cause the damage she was trying to do.

Courtney had no choice but to call Adriana's mother and their grandmother. Being who she was, her grandmother made sure the clinic took care of what the injuries did not.

* * *

Driving to Justus and Cilicia's house was an automatic response for Adriana. She had been so lost in her emotions and memories of Jamie it took entering the Bailey's driveway for her to focus on what she should be doing. She took a deep breath as she opened her car door and carefully slid out of the driver's seat. She checked her front, left pocket to ensure she had the house keys Cilicia gave her to use in an emergency.

She took long strides up the walkway to the front door. She rang the doorbell and listened for footsteps. A minute had passed before she rang the doorbell a second time. Less than a minute later she rang a third time. No response.

Adriana knew Cilicia had the app on her phone that notified her when someone was at her front door. "She would've called me by now," Adriana thought to herself.

She decided not to ring the doorbell a fourth time; she just used her key.

Adriana gently pushed open the door with her left arm as she peered inside the home. She tipped onto the Mahogany wood floors, trying to listen for voices or the television or any sign someone was home. She looked to her left then to her right. She walked down the hallway that led to the family room and kitchen.

"Cilicia," Adriana said when she saw her friend standing by the island that separated the kitchen from the family room.

Cilicia did not respond to her name being called. She seemed transfixed by something. Adriana called her again then slowly approached the area where she was standing.

Adriana saw what had Cilicia's attention.

She looked at Cilicia, "What did you do?"

"The crazy bitch stabbed me!" Justus answered.

"DO NOT SAY ANOTHER FING WORD," Cilicia said with a sternness in her voice Adriana had never heard.

Fear began to consume Adriana. She knew all too well what this could lead to.

"Say another word and you are a DEAD Bastard!" Cilicia promised.

Adriana pushed her way between Cilicia and the corner of the island that separated her from her husband. She tried to make eye contact, but Cilicia looked past her and continued to stare at Justus.

"Cilicia, give me the knife," Adriana requested in a very calm voice. She reached for the knife.

Cilicia turned to look at Adriana then back at her husband whose pants were pulled to his knees with blood dripping from his penis.

Justus lifted his hips off the floor then slid backwards.

"I said DO NOT MOVE!" Cilicia informed him.

Adriana looked at Justus then Cilicia. She looked back at Justus who was clearly frightened. Fear was something she had never seen in him.

Adriana moved closer to Cilicia. She took two steps to her left hoping to break Cilicia's stare. She laid her left hand on Cilicia shoulder. She leaned to whisper in her right ear.

"Please, Cilicia, give me the knife. Whatever it is, he is not worth it," were her words as she slid her left-hand down Cilicia's arm to get the knife.

Cilicia looked into Adriana's eyes. All emotion had seemed to be gone from Cilicia. Cilicia took a deep, sobbing breath as she surrendered the knife. She looked away from Adriana and shook her head. Life seemed to be leaving her body.

"Where are the kids?" Adriana asked no one in particular.

Cilicia looked at Justus as if she was daring him to speak.

"They are at a band competition," Cilicia's cold voice answered.

"Where?" Adriana asked.

Cilicia was still staring at her husband with tears rolling down her cheeks.

Justus was now standing and leaning against the kitchen cabinets.

Cilicia turned to Adriana with a certain coldness in her eyes.

"Columbia," Cilicia answered.

"When will they be back?" Adriana questioned.

"I'm not sure; they rode to the school with one of their friends," Cilicia answered. "What time is it?" she asked, turning her head to search within the kitchen for the answer.

Cilicia looked at Justus. "He's fucking Gavin."

Those words hit Adriana like a freight train. She felt her stomach come into her throat. She looked at Cilicia then Justus.

"TELL HER, JUSTUS. You're fucking Gavin," Cilicia had steeled her body for another confrontation. She raised her right arm into the air, extended her index finger, then pointed to her husband. "SO HELP YOU, GOD! TELL HER!"

"CILICIA, STOP THIS!" Justus demanded. "You don't know what you're talking about."

Adriana felt as if her world had ended. She looked at Justus and then Cilicia. She wanted to leave them in their hell, but she was too paralyzed to move.

"I can't get him to come to bed at night, but I can catch him jacking off looking at gay porn," Cilicia said.

Justus looked at Cilicia with rage, "FOR ONCE IN YOUR LIFE, SHUT THE FUCK UP!"

Justus's voice snapped Adriana out of her trance. She looked at him but saw Jamie. She looked down at the knife she was still holding.

"Help me," Adriana whispered as she tried to calm the tempest that was beginning to brew.

She looked at Justus and saw his weakness. She looked at Cilicia and tightened her grip on the knife. She bit her lower lip.

Adriana looked at Cilicia again, "Let's go!" she insisted.

"I'm not going anywhere," Cilicia announced. Then she pointed her left forefinger at Justus. "He will have to go," she announced in a diabolical way.

"I ain't going nowhere," Justus said to Cilicia leaning forward to reinforce his point.

"Justus," Adriana turned to him with disdain. "Please," she begged him through gritted teeth.

"No!" Justus said. "This is my house!"

Adriana looked at Cilicia, placed her hand on her chest, then gave a slight push towards the foyer. "Please, come with me, Cilicia. Please," she pleaded.

"LEAVE," Cilicia yelled to Justus. "JUST LEAVE! You don't want me! You're tired of the kids! You want to be free! Just leave!" she yelled.

Adriana pleaded with Cilicia still nudging her towards the door. "You can come to my house."

"If I leave," Cilicia said, "I'm staying in the secret apartment I just found out about."

"Just be quiet," Justus said, throwing his hands into the air.

"If I leave this house," Cilicia replied to Justus, "I will leave going to your secret apartment. I wonder what I will find there." She took a step forward, causing Adriana to step back.

"Stay away from my stuff if you plan on living," Justus informed Cilicia with anger Adriana had never seen in his eyes.

Adriana pushed Cilicia again. Everything in her wanted to leave them in their pandemonium, but she didn't want to deal with the possible aftermath of what they did to each other if she left.

"Or what?" Cilicia challenged him. Justus dropped his head. He had pulled his pants up, but blood was seeping through.

"Justus, you need to go to the hospital," Adriana said.

Justus looked down at his pants. "I'll be all right," he said. "This isn't the first time she's done crazy shit. Just take the bitch with you." Justus threw his hands towards the door.

Cilicia walked towards Justus. Adriana used every force within her to hold Cilicia back.

"I hate you," Cilicia informed Justus, then reached around Adriana and pushed Justus further into the cabinets.

Adriana became paralyzed as Justus's right arm raised, and his hand tightened around his wife's neck.

"JUSTUS, STOP!" Adriana yelled. She pushed him as hard as she could.

"JUSTUS!" she yelled again.

Justus dropped his arm. Cilicia began to cough; she massaged her neck. They stared at each other.

Adriana looked at Justus, "If she won't leave, then you leave."

Justus and Cilicia continued their staring match.

Adriana finally managed to move Cilicia to put some distance between the couple. She faced Cilicia.

"Somebody's got to have some sense here," Adriana said. "Damnit,

Cilicia. Let's go." She pushed Cilicia out of the kitchen and into the family room.

Cilicia stopped resisting and walked to the car with Adriana. Adriana left the premises as quickly as she could.

"I'm getting you a hotel room," Adriana said. "We can't go to my house right now."

"He hasn't touched me in over four years," Cilicia said with tears rolling down her face. "Four years!"

Adriana didn't know what to say. That was a reality she could not understand. She couldn't be naked around Gavin without him wanting to touch her and make love. They had never gone more than a week without sex other than the times she had given birth. Even then, she gave him oral sex at least twice during those six weeks.

"What time will the kids be back?" Adriana asked, needing to change the subject. "Do we need to get them?"

"They carpooled to school to go to band competition," Cilicia uttered in a low voice.

"What time are you expecting them back? They don't need to go home tonight," Adriana advised.

Cilicia didn't respond. She continued to stare out the window as if she was looking into another world. Adriana glanced at her trying to decide what to do.

Adriana called her mom to ask if Alexus and Evian could come over.

Adriana paused.

"Things are little complicated right now," Adriana said to her mom.

Another pause.

"I probably won't be home tonight. Please let the kids know they will be sharing their rooms."

Adriana tapped Cilicia on her arm. "Cilicia, text Alexus and tell her to go to my house when they get back from the competition.

Make-up something about you and Justus being on a date or something," Adriana instructed her.

Cilicia wasn't responding as quickly as Adriana wanted her to. She was still looking at the sky. Adriana began to panic.

"Pull up her number," Adriana instructed, handing Cilicia the phone she had put on her lap. Adriana saw it lying on the table in the foyer as they were leaving and brought it with them.

Cilicia accepted the phone, pulled up Alexus's number, and handed the phone back to Adriana without looking at her.

Adriana quickly texted Alexus the message.

"When will u b home?" Alexus questioned back.

"I will come get you," Adriana responded back.

"R U okay?" Alexus texted back.

"Yes," was the response.

"He's on pills and coke, too, you know," Cilicia broke her silence.

Adriana didn't respond. Sheraton had made comments a couple of years ago about concerns Winston had about Justus's finances. Adriana never told Cilicia concerns Sheraton had and vice versa. She was simply their ear in troubled times.

"We can talk about it when we get to the hotel," Adriana said to Cilicia. She simply wanted to get her friend to safety as quickly as possible.

She picked up her phone that was lying in the center console. She dialed Gavin's number.

"Get over to Justus and Cilicia's house now!" she demanded.

There was a momentary pause.

"Just get over here now," she said.

She looked down at Cilicia's phone. "Okay, the kids are going to spend tonight at our house."

Adriana drove the next few minutes in silence. She wanted to escape this reality as much as she wanted to get Cilicia away from her house.

"Adriana, I'm serious about what I said in the house," Cilicia said. "I saw a naked picture of Gavin on Justus's phone."

Adriana did not respond. She could not respond. She did not want to think about what Cilicia had said when she first entered the kitchen. If Adriana allowed herself to think about what Cilicia had said, she just might do something to her herself.

So, she blocked it out of her mind. All she wanted and needed to do was get them both to safety.

"I've been trying to make it work," Cilicia said. "He just keeps making things worse. He hasn't touched me in over four years. He won't get up for me, but I see pictures of him screwing other people. He got up today when he was jacking off to a picture of Gavin. I hate him for doing this to me," she said through her tears.

Finally, Adriana spoke, "Just shut up about that, Cilicia! I don't want to hear another word about Gavin. This is between you and Justus!" Adriana shot a look at her as if they were daggers piercing her soul.

Cilicia was so out of it; she barely heard what Adriana said and missed her look she gave her.

"Everything just keeps getting worse. He's a fucking accountant, and we don't have any money. I had to ask my dad for money last month, my mom the month before that. God knows what will happen this month," Cilicia said.

Adriana placed her left elbow on the driver's door, then rested her hand on her forehead. She shook her head. She was in an abyss and without a way out. She felt trapped.

She had driven two and half miles down the boulevard listening to Cilicia's agony while trying to deal with her own conundrum; one that was not created by anything she had done, but one created by innuendo.

"When I confronted him about our sex life, he told me to just get a boyfriend." Cilicia looked at Adriana. "Who in their right mind tells their wife to get a fucking boyfriend? He stopped going to church with us. He acts like attending the kids' activities are a burden on him," Cilicia continued through her tears.

Cilicia wept and sobbed. Adriana reached into the lower compartment of her door and unsympathetically handed Cilicia some napkins.

Cilicia wiped her face. "He even told me that he never wanted to get married and have children. Why, Adriana? Why did he ask me to marry him? Why did he let me fall in love with him if he knew that about himself? He could've saved us both a lot of misery."

Adriana sat in silence because she could not answer that question. She had questions of her own about her marriage.

"Where are we going?" Cilicia asked as Adriana entered the interstate.

"We're taking a drive," Adriana answered. She was still trying to process everything that had happened in the past thirty minutes. She needed to calm her own nerves.

"My marriage has been over for a while now. I just didn't want to accept it," Cilicia confessed.

Cilicia sobbed. Adriana looked over at her with a mixture of hatred and pity.

"I thought that if I gave him some time and space, he would see how much he loved the kids and me," Cilicia continued. "It seemed that the more I tried to love him and give him space, the worse he got." The tears would not stop coming.

Adriana glanced over at Cilicia. "When it gets this bad, you might be right to leave," Adriana said, something she wanted to tell her years ago.

The image of Justus standing by the cabinets with blood seeping through his pants flashed through Adriana's mind.

"Cilicia, I'm afraid for you. Violence is never good. What did you do to him?"

"I stabbed him in his penis," Cilicia admitted. "He was jacking off watching gay porn and looking at Gavin's penis, so I stabbed him. I stabbed him because he rejects me, his wife."

Adriana was still trying to contain her anger. How dare Cilicia say the things about Gavin that she was saying. How dare she bring her husband into their problems.

Cilicia crying filled the silence.

"I've wondered for years if he might be bisexual," Cilicia admitted. "I've suspected it since before Evian was born."

Adriana wanted to melt in her seat. She would never have the courage to say those words out loud about Gavin.

"Cilicia, how bad is it? How bad did you hurt him?"

"I stabbed him a couple times."

Adriana's phone rang. She looked down and saw it was Gavin calling. She didn't want to talk to him, but she answered anyway.

She listened to questions Gavin was asking her; however, she didn't provide a response to any. Given everything that was still going on, she kept the conversation brief.

"I'll talk to you later," she eventually said to her husband. She was afraid to say anything to him that she might later regret, so she ended the conversation.

"Justus is okay," she informed Cilicia.

The pair drove a few more miles in silence.

"Let's go to that apartment," Cilicia said. "I got the key." She pulled a key out of her bra.

Adriana was not ready to face the apartment. She was not ready to let Cilicia know what she knew about her own husband. She was not ready to confront that part of the truth. She was not ready to possibly relive the experience she had with Jamie. She had learned from her previous two relationships that when a man feels threatened, he will do whatever he had to do to protect himself and his image.

She recalled something Grandma Ethel told her after the situation with Jamie. *"Never pierce a man's armor. Once you do, you he never the same, and your relationship is forever changed."*

Fear, anxiety, and depression began to consume Adriana. Single parenting. Byron. Jamie. Jamie. Jamie. Gavin. She could not think about it anymore.

"I've got the key, Adriana. We need to use it," Cilicia said with a certain forcefulness.

"Are you sure that is what you want to do, Cilicia?" Adriana inquired.

"I've had enough of him. You don't know the half," Cilicia answered.

Deep down inside, Adriana knew Cilicia's marriage was over; there was no coming back from what had happened in the kitchen. But just in case a miracle was going to happen, Adriana didn't want Cilicia to put the final nail in the coffin.

"Listen to me. Once you open that door, things will forever change. You can't play with something like that."

"Things have already forever changed for me. I tried to cut off his penis for God's sake," Cilicia said throwing her hands in the air.

"Why do you think I did that? It's over between us, and I don't want him to have the pleasure of giving someone else what he wouldn't give me!" Cilicia admitted.

Adriana closed her eyes for a split second; she took a deep breath.

"We are going into this hotel and getting a room for the night. I am not going to that apartment, Cilicia."

"Why, Adriana. Explain to me why you don't want to go," Cilicia pleaded.

"Because I don't have the problems with Gavin that you have with Justus. Because I am not planning to leave my husband. At least not today," Adriana affirmed.

She looked at Cilicia with empathy and concern.

"The things you say about Justus do not apply to Gavin. He comes home when he is not working. He takes care of our children, our home. He makes me feel like he loves me. I can't just give that up; I don't want to give that up," Adriana said.

"He is cheating on you, Adriana. Gavin is cheating on you. Hell! He might even be fucking MY husband," Cilicia reiterated to her with a slap to her chest.

Adriana looked at Cilicia. "Let me make myself clear. Keep Gavin's name out of your mouth. Neither of us know if that is true," Adriana argued back with her.

"Okay," Cilicia said. "Let's go the apartment and find out. All the proof you need will be there. I promise you!" Cilicia said, looking Adriana directly and sternly in her eyes.

"YOU," Adriana began challenging Cilicia with the same look she was receiving, "might be ready to break up your home, but I am not ready to break up mine."

"What more do you need to leave his ass?" Cilicia put forward.

"Just like you, I have my limits, and you are pushing them," Adriana informed her.

"Then what are they?" Cilicia asked.

"Whenever you called me complaining about Justus, I never advised you to leave. I never encouraged you to stay if you didn't want to. I have respected every decision you made about your marriage, and you will respect the decisions I make about mine," Adriana said in a serious manner.

Cilicia looked at Adriana. She was at a loss for words.

"You can't even imagine how I'm feeling right now," Cilicia said.

"You don't know what I can imagine," Adriana informed her. "You don't know what I've been through in my life. Although I have sympathy for you and your situation, I don't know what I would do if I were in your shoes."

She looked at Cilicia with a mixture of frustration and sympathy.

"Gavin is not my first rodeo, you know," she continued as she closed her eyes and took a deep breath.

Memories of her past caused her to lift her back off the seat. She looked her distraught friend in her eyes.

"Cilicia, you frighten me when you get mad. It is as if you go into a rage when you get angry. If you and Justus continue with this violence, somebody WILL get hurt."

"I never should have married him," Cilicia whispered loud enough for Adriana to hear. "I was warned not to marry him."

"What?" Adriana asked.

"The first time he hit me was a month before our wedding, right after the invitations had been mailed out. I was standing on a ladder trying to put dishes away. He didn't like the way I talked to him, so he kicked the ladder and made me fall. I got up and slapped the shit out of him. Then he punched me in my stomach and ribs," Cilicia shared a secret she had been carrying.

Tears rolled out of Cilicia's eyes. The anger Adriana had shown towards Cilicia was beginning to feel like sorrow.

"I was too embarrassed to tell anybody what had happened. He kept calling me and apologizing for hitting me, and I believed he was sorry." Cilicia continued.

"I let him come to my hotel room and talk about it. He agreed to go to counseling, so that's what we did. At the end of our second session, the therapist advised me not to marry him. She told me to cancel the wedding and forgot about the money I had already spent. She said that marrying him would cost me a whole lot more later."

Cilicia said staring into the distance. "I thought she was talking about money. Now I know she was talking about soul."

Adriana looked over at Cilicia. She didn't know what to say or do.

"She told me that some women experience domestic violence for the first time when they are pregnant. She told me that Justus exhibited characteristics of someone who would abuse me again," Cilicia kept going.

"I had no idea," Adriana said.

"The next time he hit me was the night we buried my grandmother. Remember, you and Gavin were on your honeymoon when she passed," Cilicia said making eye contact with Adriana for a moment.

"I remember," Adriana said feeling her own rage calming down.

"He said that I was taking my grandmother's death too seriously and acting like a baby. He kept mocking me and getting in my face. I pushed him and tried to walk out of the house. That's when he grabbed me by the neck and told me I wasn't going anywhere. Then he slapped me," Cilicia said with a certain distance and coldness.

"That was the night I made up my mind to fight his ass back and to get him before he got me," Cilicia said.

Adriana looked upon her friend with sympathy and confusion.

"He fears me just as much as I fear him," Cilicia said.

"What about the children?" Adriana asked.

"Most of the time they don't see us fighting," Cilicia answered.

"Cilicia, what are you teaching your children?" Adriana asked. "Do you want this for them?"

"That's why I'm leaving him," Cilicia said with sadness. "I can't let my children continue to think this is how a marriage is supposed to be."

For the first time in this saga, Adriana began to feel compassion for Cilicia. Then she became lost in the vague memory she had of the day her mother left her father.

She was six when her mother took her and her older brothers to live with their grandmother, who welcomed them with open arms because she had been living alone since the death of their grandfather.

Adriana stayed with her grandmother until she went to college. She decided not to leave her grandmother after her mother's remarriage. She remembered how lost she felt once her parents separated and feeling as if she was the reason their marriage failed.

"When was the last time you went to counseling?" Adriana inquired.

"Adriana," Cilicia said with tears in her eyes, "did you not hear with I just told you. Counseling does not work for everyone. Justus wants me to take responsibility for his actions and mine."

"I didn't know," Adriana said.

"We've been to several counselors. Nothing ever got better with us. I suggested we try a male counselor a few years ago. He refused to go. The last time we went to counseling, he refused to do his personal sessions before we returned to couple's therapy. I've tried everything, Adriana. Nothing has worked," Cilicia informed.

Adriana needed to settle her nerves. She left Cilicia in the car while she purchased a room. The walk to the hotel lobby was grueling. Seeing Justus choke Cilicia had impacted her more than she realized. Tears were starting to well up in her eyes.

"You can't do this right now," she told herself. "Get yourself together."

She straightened her back, sucked her stomach in, and pulled her shoulders back. She approached the counter.

Ten minutes later she was returning to her car.

"Okay; we can go in," she informed Cilicia.

Cilicia got out of the car and followed Adriana until they reached their room.

"I got water when I checked us in," Adriana said, offering Cilicia a bottle.

Adriana sat on the bed near the window. She looked upon the

skyline that had changed since her wedding day. Everything had changed in the city she found peace in. So much had changed in the mind of the young woman who would soon be celebrating her eighteenth wedding anniversary.

As Adriana got lost in her past, Cilicia walked into the bathroom.

* * *

Adriana awakened from her sleep. She rose from her bed. She didn't see Cilicia in the bed next to her. She knocked on the bathroom door. Cilicia didn't answer. She checked the handle, then pushed the door slightly open.

"I'm going to get something to eat. What do you want?"

Cilicia didn't answer. Adriana called her name. No answer.

Adriana walked into the bathroom to make sure she was still in there and had not fallen asleep. She noticed the limpness of her right arm.

"Cilicia! Cilicia!" Adriana frantically tried to awaken her. She leaned into Cilicia's face to place her ear to her nose. She was still breathing.

Adriana went back into the room to call the front desk for help. Then she used her cell phone to call 9-1-1.

Hotel personnel used their own to key to enter the room. Adriana explained to them that she didn't know what was wrong with Cilicia. Several questions were asked of her as notes were taken on a tablet.

Minutes later, there was another knock on the door. The man from the hotel opened the door.

"She's in here," Adriana called to the emergency personnel. "She's still breathing."

Adriana stood and observed from the doorway as Cilicia's almost lifeless body was lifted out of the bathtub.

"How long has she been like this?" the male asked.

"An hour and half at the most," Adriana answered; that was around the time she had fallen asleep.

"What's her name?" the female worker asked.

"Cilicia Bailey," Adriana answered.

"Cilicia, this is Shavonda. Can you tell me what you took?"

Memories of her own suicide attempt came into Adriana mind. She began to feel scared.

"What happened?" came the next question from the male.

"She had a fight with her husband. I brought her here to put some distance between them. I sat on the bed, and she went into the bathroom. I woke up and was going to get us something to eat when I found her."

"Do you know what she took?" the male asked.

"I didn't know she had anything," Adriana answered.

"We'll need to transport her to the hospital," Adriana heard the woman in the bathroom say.

Adriana's phone rang. It was Gavin.

"May I answer this? It's my husband," Adriana asked.

The male nodded.

Adriana kept her conversation short with Gavin. She informed him that Cilicia was being transported to the hospital and that she would call her mother.

"Are you still with Justus?" she asked.

There was a pause.

"I don't think you need to bring him right now."

There was another pause.

"I'll talk to you about it when I get home," Adriana said.

Adriana paced the floor. The woman exited the bathroom.

"Your friend is going to be okay," she informed Adriana. "She will need to get some help to get through whatever is going on with her."

"A bad marriage," Adriana said.

Another team of emergency workers arrived with a stretcher. The first male on the scene briefed the second team.

"I need to get some information from you," the female worker said.

Adriana answered the questions as best she could.

"She'll be at Atrium," one of the males from the second team said on his way out the door.

In the Eye of the Hurricane

I am at it again;
Life is leaving me.

Then I am in the eye where things seem clear;
The cyclone is necessary to stir things up;
While the wind and rain bring
Nutrients that could not have otherwise made their way inland.

As I look to my help;
I see the rainbow;
Life is possible after the storm.

14

The Eye of the Storm

Adriana was a couple of minutes behind the ambulance. Memories of the days she had contemplated or attempted suicide clouded her mind. The first time she had thought about suicide was when she was eleven. Her older brother had been playing with her in the middle of the night since she was in kindergarten. It first started with her touching his lightsaber then it progressed to her seeing how many licks it took to get to the pop.

When he came home from college for Thanksgiving break, he started preparing her for the real world. That was the first time she had taken a bottle of aspirin; something inside of her knew he was taking IT too far. She remembered feeling like something was wrong in elementary school, but her brother kept telling her that secrets were not bad things to keep. He told her that he kept a lot of secrets and wanted her to learn from him instead of somebody else. But that Thanksgiving break when she was eleven years old left her feeling ashamed because there was blood. Blood always meant something bad had happened.

She thought about suicide the last time she had seen Byron. Being alone in that hotel room had her questioning her value. If she had not been headed back to college, away from the reality that she had promised to change for the children she would one day have, she might have attempted suicide then.

So much about the drive to the hospital had Adriana nerves in a bundle. Was there nothing in Cilicia's life to live for? Her children, perhaps? Her career? Then she thought about her students' essays and how one student condemned the poet for not fighting for herself, her children, and her career; the student had thought the poet's life might have saved her son.

Adriana thought about Cilicia's value. Although she had been infuriated with her the past year, she could not imagine her life without her.

Then she thought about the poet again. Could Cilicia have a mental health issue that was just manifesting? Or was her life with Justus so bad that it had triggered a mental breakdown. She had not seen Cilicia's accusations as a cry for help; she had felt that Cilicia was trying to pull her into the mounting drama between her and Justus.

Adriana parked her car. She hurried from the parking garage into the emergency room. She explained to the check-in clerk why she was there. He informed her that she needed to check-in before getting an update.

Adriana called her mother to give a rundown of everything that had happened since she left home earlier in the day. She reluctantly called Gavin to tell him where she was and what had happened.

With even more reluctance, she called Cilicia's mother. She skirted around the truth, giving just enough information to make her aware of the seriousness of what had happened.

Adriana felt so alone and confused. There was no one in her world who she could trust enough to talk to about what was really going on. She didn't want to talk to her mother because she didn't want to change her mother's perception of Gavin and Justus.

Adriana began to recognize the urgency of needing to speak with someone inside herself. She was trying to hold on to the last bit of sanity she had left; she was spiraling fast and furious; she had felt these feelings before but never at the same time. She realized there was one step between how she was feeling and where Cilicia was. She let the tears go.

One of the women behind the check-in counter recognized what was happening. She escorted Adriana to a room. She brought water to her.

"Do you need to be admitted?" she asked.

Adriana shook her head. She was hyperventilating.

"Is there someone I can call for you?"

Again, Adriana shook her head. The woman left her in the room.

Adriana allowed the tears that had become anger flow. What would she do if Gavin was in a sexual relationship with Justus? What if everything Cilicia said was true? How would she handle that truth?

"Oh, God. I can't do this. I didn't sign up for this. What have I done to deserve this? Me," Adriana cried in a low voice. "I feel so betrayed, so confused. What…did…I…do?"

Adriana was disrupted by the woman's return to the room.

"There is a man out here asking about your friend," the woman said, taking notice of Adriana's condition.

"He says he is her husband."

Adriana wiped her face. "Give me a few minutes to get myself together. I'll be right out."

Adriana decided to call Athra. She needed prayer, wisdom, and strength. She needed the father, the son, and the holy spirit to give her what she needed to face Justus.

Before Adriana could reach the waiting room where Justus was, the male attendant informed her that Cilicia was asking for her. Adriana's eyes looked at the ceiling. She cupped her hands together and thanked God for giving her a few more minutes to get herself together.

"Lead me; guide me; protect me," she prayed out loud. The gentleman nodded his head as he used his badge to let her into the area where Cilicia was being treated.

The emergency room was a busy place. Adriana followed the clerk to the nurse's station.

"They will help you from here," he informed her.

"I'm here to see Cilicia Bailey," Adriana told the nurse sitting behind the desk.

The nurse rose from her desk and looked around Adriana.

"Do you see that nurse over there?" she asked, pointing to a nurse standing in front of sliding glass door; "She can help you."

Adriana proceeded to the door where the nurse was standing.

"Excuse, me." Adriana said waiting for the nurse to make eye contact with her. "I'm here to see Cilicia Bailey."

The nurse looked at Adriana's distraught face, "She's in here," then she escorted her into the room next to where she was standing.

Adriana walked into the room. She looked at the monitors that then followed their leads into Cilicia. She straightened her face as she slowly walked to the bed. Adriana looked at Cilicia. She wanted to ask her so many questions to understand what had happened, but she chose not to.

Cilicia looked at Adriana. She could see the distress in her face; she could see the streaks left by the tears; she knew by her quivering lip she was trying to hold it together. Cilicia turned her face back to the wall.

"The hospital is going to admit me for observation," Cilicia informed Adriana in a low, raspy voice.

"Okay; how long will you be here?"

"They are going to keep me for at least three days, maybe longer." Cilicia said, who had turned onto her back but still struggling to look Adriana in her face.

"I have a favor to ask," Cilicia timidly said, turning her face away from where Adriana stood.

"What do you need?" Adriana asked.

"I need you to keep my children while I'm here. I don't want them with Justus. I don't want them with my parents. I need to know they are safe while I'm here," Cilicia said with tears in her voice. She wiped her eyes.

"I don't have a problem keeping them," Adriana said. Being their godmother, she made a promise before God and everyone in the church to take care of Alexus and Evian in the event Cilicia and Justus couldn't. That day was upon her.

"How will Justus feel about it?" Thoughts of what she witnessed earlier caused her to feel anxious about making the request a reality.

"If he disagrees with you, tell him I said that I will tell his parents everything. He doesn't want his parents to feel ashamed of him, so he will comply," Cilcicia said with certainty.

There was something in Cilicia's voice that made Adriana feel she was speaking to a woman who was getting ready for war.

"He's in the waiting room."

"I don't want to see him; I have given him enough of me. I need to take care of myself right now."

"Cilicia."

"They are carrying me to the sixth floor for observation." Cilicia was feeling dejected. The image of Alexus standing at the top of the stairs and imagining what she had witnessed along with the past several months had drained the life out of Cilicia.

"Take care of my children, Adriana, Please."

"I'm their godmother, Cilicia; of course, I'll take care of them," Adriana promised.

CONFUSION, COMPASSION, CONFESSION ~ 117

Adriana looked at her phone. Two text messages had come through.

"Cilicia, do you remember my friend Athra?"

"Vaguely."

"I called her. I asked her to come and pray for you. She's in the waiting room now."

"Why would you do that?" Cilicia asked, feeling as if her privacy had been violated.

"Athra is a minister now. I trust her, Cilicia. She's been helping me deal with all of this," Adriana exposed the secret she had been keeping for the past couple of months.

Cilicia turned and looked at Adriana. Something about Adriana's acknowledgment brought relief to Cilicia.

"Do they allow two people in the room?" Cilicia asked.

"I don't know. She can come while I go to the waiting room to talk to Justus."

Cilicia was apprehensive about letting someone else in this space. She didn't know if she wanted prayer because she wasn't sure she wanted to be here. She didn't know if she could face her daughter and her parents. What could she say to Alexus if she witnessed what Justus had done to her.

"I'm not ready for that right now," Cilicia finally said to Adriana.

"Cilicia, listen to me," Adriana paused. "I know how you feel; I've been here myself. Alexus and Evian need YOU. I need You. I would pray for you myself, but I don't know if it would have the same effect."

Cilicia turned and looked at Adriana. She began to cry. Something in Adriana's voice told Cilicia they could get past this, which was another reason for her distress.

"Why did you come to the house?"

"Sheraton called and said you didn't show up for an appointment, and you weren't answering your phone."

Cilicia's heart dropped even further. She began to feel more guilty. Why had she opened Pandora's box?

Adriana noticed the look. "Just let Athra pray for you, Cilicia, please."

Cilicia thought about her parents and the damnation she would receive if they knew what she had done. She could only imagine the type of redemptative treatment she would receive from them. She didn't want to see a hospital chaplain because they would be traditionalist like her parents. A million thoughts kept invading her mind.

"Just this once," Cilicia said, mainly out of guilt for what she was doing to Adriana right now.

Adriana left the room. She stopped at the nurse's station and was informed only one visitor at a time. She also learned that most people in Cilicia's situation are held for at least three days in observation.

Adriana pushed the handicap button to automatically open the doors. She sauntered to the waiting room thinking about how she would manage this crisis; she was surprised to see Gavin talking to Athra. Justus was sitting in a chair next to where Gavin was standing with his forehead in his hand.

Gavin noticed the change in Athra's face and turned to see Adriana. He met his wife and gave her a hug; she pushed him away. For the first time in their marriage, Gavin's toned body and his presence didn't give her a sense of security. Gavin looked at her with uncertainty.

Adriana wasn't sure what she was feeling for Gavin. Again, Gavin put his arms around Adriana and pulled her towards him with a little more force. He tightened his arms around her and rested his chin on her head.

When Adriana opened her eyes, they met Justus; he dropped his head. She pushed away from her husband then walked to Athra.

"Cilicia has agreed to allow you to pray for her."

Athra patted her on her hand then went to see Cilicia.

Justus stood up. "How is Cilicia?"

Anger welled up in Adriana. "How dare you ask about her!" is what she yelled in her mind. "You deserve nothing, you bastard. I hate you!"

She looked at Gavin then Justus. "She's okay," Adriana said. "She doesn't want to see you right now; it will be a few days."

"Why a few days?" Justus asked.

"She is staying here for observation."

"Why?" Gavin asked.

"She attempted suicide."

15

My Love is Too Delicaate

Adriana was happy Gavin talked to Justus about the kids; that was one headache she didn't have to worry about. As soon as she walked into the family room, the children came rushing to her. She could read the questions in their eyes.

"Your mom had a little accident. The hospital is going to keep her for a few days," she told them.

Alexus looked at her then walked away. A part of Adriana's heart dropped; there was nothing she could do to help the teenager at that moment.

"What happened?" Evian inquired.

Although the younger teenager was eye level to Adriana, the innocence was still there. She would bet that Alexus had protected him as much as she could from the reality of their parents' relationship.

"She was in the bathtub and accidentally fell asleep. Water got in her lungs, so they need to keep a close watch on her for the next few days to make sure she doesn't have any more problems," Adriana explained to him.

Alexus looked at Adriana with suspicion but didn't question what Evian had been told.

"When do we get to go see her?" Evian asked.

"She will call us and let us know." She gave him a side hug and kiss on his forehead. He returned to the table with Ariadne and Nicklous and put his head down.

"Mama," Nicklous walked up to his mother, "is Mrs. Cilicia going to be okay?"

"Yes; you don't need to worry about her." She looked over at Evian. "All you need to do is be nice and share your room with Evian."

Nicklous laid his head on his mother's shoulder. She embraced him and gave him a kiss on his forehead, too.

Adriana walked over to the stove where Regenia was cooking. "It never fails," she said to her mother.

The meal Regenia was cooking - fried and baked chicken, macaroni and cheese, fresh string beans, cornbread, pound cake, and sweet tea – told Adriana that her mother had been in prayer and meditation over the situation with Cilicia.

Regenia walked over to Adriana. "You know that girl does not believe what you told her brother," Regenia whispered to Adriana. "She talked to me since she's been here. She's been scared all day."

"Why was she scared?" Adriana asked.

"We'll talk about it later," Regenia said looking in the distance to Alexus.

Adriana was too exhausted to question her mother about the look. A part of her didn't want to learn the truth about her mother's pain. Grandma Gina used to say from time to time, "Let sleeping dogs lie;" and this time those dogs might have needed to remain six feet deep.

Nicklous and Evian helped Adriana set the table. She asked Evian about the band competition. Evian was happy to share that NaFo had received a "Superior" rating.

When Gavin came into the kitchen, Justus followed him. Evian walked over to his father and spoke to him. Justus greeted his son back.

"Mrs. Adriana said Mama wants us to stay here while she's in the hospital," Evian said.

Justus looked Evian in the eyes, "Yes. Your mama needs some time to get better, and I need to focus on taking care of her. You and your sister will stay here while your mom gets better."

Alexus looked at her father. She walked away to another room.

Regenia noticed that Justus was about to follow Alexus. "She's worried about her mama. I think she needs a little space."

Justus stopped and looked at the grandmother. Although he wanted to pursue his daughter, his upbringing and guilt made him listen to her advice.

"We better eat," Regenia said. She turned on the television and found a football game. She didn't instruct the children to put their phones down as they ate their food and checked their social media accounts. She needed time to process everything that was happening, too.

* * *

Adriana retreated to her bedroom once everyone in the house was settled. She was so happy her mother was staying. She needed the anchor while she worked through her own dilemma. Her presence and strength would be needed to help Alexus and Evian get through these next few days.

Adriana stood under the shower to let the water wash away the stress she was feeling. She allowed the tears to flow once again. She wanted to break down.

She recalled Courtney's words to her when she was released from the hospital after her suicide attempt, "You're a Black woman, and Black woman don't break. You're stronger than this."

Adriana thought about the people in her home. She thought about her grandmothers and their mothers. Since recorded time, women have been pillars of strength. "We might bend, but we never break," her grandmother told her when she attempted suicide.

Adriana reached for her mittens then lathered them. She began with her neck then scrubbed down to get rid of some of the pain. Underneath the top layer of pain was what she thought she needed to get through the night.

The pain of the abuse she felt the night Bryon beat her was closer to the surface than she wanted to feel. Justus reaching around her to choke Cilicia caused her to relive the experience of Bryon trying to take her life.

Then Cilicia's words, "He's fucking Gavin," rang from her left ear to her right ear. They bounced from the right hemisphere to the left. But they were only words. She could not conjure an image of Gavin being with another man. For a moment, she was grateful to have the image of Blair giving him a blow job.

Then she saw Jamie, lying on his stomach with his hips in the air. If she confronted Gavin, would he react the same way Jamie had? Would she have to explain to her children and their mothers why they divorced when everything seemed to be going so well?

Did it matter if Gavin was having sex with a man or woman? Infidelity was the same regardless of gender. Was it the fact he was away from home three or four days a week that made their marriage beautiful? Or was it the fact that Gavin was able to live life on his terms instead of hers? What were her terms? Were they different than what she had been living? She had so many questions with no clear answers.

"Justus and Cilicia's business is not our business," Gavin, who was sitting on the bed, said to his wife when she walked into their bedroom.

Adriana didn't respond to him. She could see the stress and desperation on his face. She assumed Justus had informed him about the things Cilicia said before she took her away.

Adriana was still not ready to accept the things Cilicia had been saying about Gavin let alone to confront him. In the depths of her spirit, she knew that the moment she approached Gavin with accusations of infidelity, their marriage would forever be changed. The fact that Adriana believed in him so faithfully was a part of Gavin's armor. She knew she had not made the decision to alter the reality she was living in because it brought her everything she had wanted in life. She wasn't ready to probe her life into another reality. Watching Cilicia was painful enough.

Adriana looked at her husband and slid into their bed. She needed to escape this reality; she wanted to dream.

Gavin turned to look at his wife. He wanted to feel close to her; he even needed to feel close to her, so he laid on the bed and slid close to her.

"Our marriage is solid, Adriana. I don't care what Cilicia might have told you; it's not true. What's between Justus and Cilicia is between them. We don't need to put ourselves in anybody else's marriage," he beseeched his wife.

Even in this crisis, Gavin was still maintaining his cool. She thought about the catfish in Athra's aquarium – swimming slowly and peacefully at the bottom while the other fish were swimming swiftly and darting around each other.

A part of her wanted to let him know she knew about Blair and the extra phones he had, but she was too afraid to. What if he would react like Jamie or Byron? He had never acted as if he would abuse her, but neither had Jamie. What if this was the thing that would trigger something in him that maybe, even, he didn't know existed.

The lump came back into her throat and moved throughout her body. She curled up. She couldn't speak; she wanted the life she had this time last year. She wanted to believe that she was the only person in Gavin's life – the only person who felt him.

Gavin moved closer to Adriana and held her. His scent made her heart melt; his arms reminded her that he was THE man she wanted him to be – someone who would forever protect her. She felt confused and conflicted.

She thought about how Gavin and Justus had come into the house. She could see that no matter what had taken place, their friendship would never break; they would never give each other up.

Adriana began to cry. She felt guilty about her feelings towards Cilicia. She wasn't there when Cilicia was pleading for help; she had not heard what Cilicia was really saying. Cilicia needed her to listen, not as much about Gavin, but about what and how she was feeling about Justus and her marriage. She was trying to tell Adriana that she was feeling less than a woman.

Gavin put his hand on Adriana shoulder. "I love you, Adriana. You don't have to do this. I love you."

Adriana continued to ignore him. She thought about how quickly women turn on each other, more quickly than men will. She thought about how tight Gavin and Justus's bond was and how Gavin was supporting him. And here she was, ready to turn her back on Cilicia and let her deal with this alone. Could it really be their bonding through sex that allows men to take things to their graves that women would kill another for?

Gavin moved closer to Adriana and pulled her into his arms. She struggled to settle in. She wanted to resist the love Gavin was giving her because she knew she didn't have him all to herself. Yet, another part of her wanted to surrender to the security he gave her. Even in this time of uncertainty, he wanted to reassure her he would never fail her. Finally, she fell asleep.

* * *

The next five days went smoother than Adriana had expected. Regenia had given up her room to Alexus; she had made the morning room her bedroom. Nicklous was happy to share his room with Evian; he had someone to play games with.

Cilicia was being discharged and would be coming home with Adriana. She was still not ready to speak to Justus, and she didn't feel safe around him. She wanted to spend some time with her children before facing him, before having to go into the theatre that would only result in destruction.

"Cilicia," Adriana began, "your mom came this morning."

Adriana noticed how Cilicia furrowed her brows and extended her chin. "Why couldn't she had waited?" Her exhaled breath got Adriana's attention.

She had always tried to understand the relationship between Cilicia and her mother. She had accepted that things were not the best between them, which is why Cilicia had been relying on her mother these past few months. There were times when Adriana wished Cilicia would not crowd their space; however, she knew her mother would not have it any other way, so she didn't make her feelings known.

Cilicia dried the tears that were in the corner of her eyes. She thanked Adriana for keeping Alexus and Evian with her. She apologized for the inconvenience and the sacrifice she knew her best friend had been making.

Adriana listened as Cilicia talked. She didn't yield her full attention to the conversation; her mind was on working through her own marriage. She decided to text Athra.

Adriana finally reached the Sanctuary; going through the entrance felt different this time. It felt like she was allowing dark spirits to enter her haven. As she drove towards her enclave, she looked in her rearview mirror. "God, let whatever this thing that has taken Cilicia be left outside of these gates."

Sadness overcame Adriana. Memories of her own fight for recovery flooded her mind. She thought about the role Cilicia played in helping her heal. "The person who assured me Gavin was a great guy is the same person trying to tear us apart," she thought.

"The beauty and the beast; the ying and the yang; the jinn," something whispered in her left ear. Adriana shook her head.

"Don't do this to yourself; don't do this to her," something whispered to her in her right ear.

"Oh, God," Adriana said to herself.

She looked over at Cilicia who had fallen asleep. She remembered the day Courtney and Grandma Gina brought her home. She remembered her unsettling feelings as if she was in another space and time. Although she was in this world, her mind and spirit were still in the place that had offered her tranquility away from this world's reality. She wondered if Cilicia felt the same.

Adriana remembered what Monica had said about people not coming back; coming back is not just a physical thing; it is also something that happens in the mind and to the spirit. She wondered how all of this would affect Cilicia emotionally and spiritually.

Evian and Nicklous were outside waiting for them. Apparently, Nicklous had been tracking them on his phone. Evian was the first to approach the car. He opened the passenger side door to let his mother out of the car. He led her into the house.

Alexus's eyes met her mother's eyes; she began to cry. Cilicia held back her tears as she reached for her daughter and pulled her into her chest. That's when her tears began to flow. The foyer was silent.

Alexus led her mother into the bedroom they would be sharing; Evian followed. Cilicia explained that she didn't want them to visit in her the hospital because she needed to get well to get back home.

Alexus told her mother that she and Regenia had cleaned the room and changed the sheets.

"Mrs. Regenia let me sleep in here while you were in the hospital," Alexus informed her mother. "We are going to share tonight."

Alexus and Evian watched as their mother took her shoes off and relaxed on the bed. They gave her a quick update on their lives while she was gone.

"Grandma wanted us to go home with her when she came, but Dad said we were going to stay here until you got out of the hospital," Evian informed his mom.

"I asked Adriana if she would take care of you until I got out. Your grandmother didn't know." Cilicia was trying to ease her son's mind.

"I thought we would spend the night at home since you are out," Evian continued.

"I need to relax before we go home, and I have to get back into mommy mode."

"When are we going home?" he asked.

"We're never going back," Alexus snapped at him. "Just leave Mama alone. She needs to rest."

"What's wrong with you," Evian turned away from his mother to face his sister. "I asked a simple question."

"Just leave her alone," Alexus demanded.

"Mama, something's been wrong with her since we came here. She barely talked to anyone on the bus when we went to the competition. She wouldn't even let Jai'Nesha sit on the seat her on the way home," Evian informed her mother.

Alexus grabbed Evian by his wrist. "Just leave her alone and let her get some rest," she instructed as she pulled him towards the door.

He yanked away from her, "Mama didn't say I have to leave. You're not my parent."

Alexus looked at her mother. Her eyes answered the question Cilicia had been asking since the night she saw her on the stairs.

"Evian, you may come back after I take a nap. My medicine is beginning to work," Cilicia said in support of her protector.

Cilicia snuggled into the bed as her children left the room. She was pleased to know that her children were happy given the circumstances. Evian informed her their father had been there every day to check on them and to eat dinner, so she decided to sleep as long as possible to avoid him.

* * *

The light woke Cilicia from her sleep. Her eye adjusted to the light as she focused in on the woman standing by her bedside. She didn't need to fully focus to know it was her mother.

"We've been praying for you, Baby," Cilicia's mother began. "We're glad you home so you and Justus can get things back right."

Cilicia turned to her mother. "Thank you for your prayers, Mama. I'm not going back to Justus."

Cilicia's mother sat on the bed near her feet. "Listen to me, girl. That man loves you and his children. He wants his family with him. You've got to help him in any way you can."

"I am helping him by leaving him, Mama," Cilicia said with tears in her voice and rolling down her cheeks.

"Men make mistakes. They get weak and slip in their faith. Remember that God forgives him, so you have to forgive him, too. It's your duty as his wife to help him pick himself up."

Cilicia sat up in the bed. "Whose duty is it to help me pick myself up every time he kicks me down?"

"That's why we got to be strong for ourselves and our husbands."

"What exactly did Justus tell you, Mama?"

"He said that he made a mistake in judgment and had a little affair. He said that he was sorry and ready for you and the kids to be back home."

Cilicia looked at her mother remembering all the times she had heard her father abuse her mother. She thought about the promises she made to herself the night her father accused her mother of not knowing how to take care of a man when her mother was trying to keep him from leaving. She heard her mother ask her father what it was that he needed that she wasn't giving him; she heard her mother unbutton his pants then heard her being pushed to the floor. She remembered how her mother was limping the next day as she cooked breakfast.

"Mama, Justus and I are over. I am not going back to him, and I'm not allowing my children to go back. Some mistakes can be forgiven but not forgotten."

"How do you think your kids are going to feel when they go to school and their parents aren't together, but all their friends' parents are? What do you think the people at church will say when they find out y'all ain't together? You got more than yourself to think about, girl."

Cilicia felt scolded and rejected. She turned her head away from her mother. She knew that she would never have her mother's support. She knew how her mother and father and the church would feel about her the moment she decided to do what was right for her and her children.

She began to softly speak, "Mama, my love is too beautiful and delicate to thrown back in my face." Then she turned and looked her mother in the eyes. "He sodomized me the day I attempted suicide, Mama. He has been sodomizing me for years instead of making love to me."

Cilicia paused, waiting for a response from her mother. Her mother did not speak; she sat looking past her daughter, showing no emotion.

"My love is too giving and forgiving to be thrown back in my face. The love I have tried to offer Justus does not belong to him because he keeps on throwing back in my face," Cilicia spoke to her mother emphasizing the words "in my face."

Cilicia sat in silence waiting for a response from her mother.

"Our daughter and your granddaughter witnessed what he did to me the last time I was in that home. I couldn't look at her when she left the house that day because I was too ashamed to face her. I love her too much to make her believe this is how a man should treat her. I am taking my love and focusing on my children because Justus has thrown it in my face for the last time."

There was silence in the room.

"If you want to see your grandchildren, you will have to come to me. I won't deal with the toxicity that my decision will bring when I visit home. I will save you the shame and keep my distance." Cilicia asserted before opening the door to leave the room.

She stopped in her tracks. She heard a sound coming from the kitchen that made her look back at her mother. As she slowly left the room, leaving her mother in her own thoughts, she deviated to the bathroom.

She leaned on the sink and looked in the mirror. "You can handle this," as she rocked back and forth. "My love is too perfect and sincere to be tossed back in my face."

She walked into the hall; she wasn't ready. She could not move forward to the place where she could find joy, and she could not go back to the room she had just left. She felt defenseless. Moving forward would mean confronting the person who had caused her so much pain; going back meant she wanted to take back what she had said to her mother.

She began to move forward and saw the morning room. She tiptoed through the sparsely lit hallway until she reached her destination. She gently placed her body on the chase lounge chair and listened to the noise coming from the kitchen. Finally, she drifted off to sleep.

16

Comfort in the Storm

Adriana realized how much she needed her session with Athra the moment she drove onto the campus. Her world had become crowded with extra people in her home. There was no place she could go within her own sanctuary to feel the connection with God that she needed during this time.

She was already snuggled up on the chaise with her blanket when Athra walked into the room. Adriana watched her in her velvet jumpsuit. The cranberry color against her caramel skin was eye-catching. Just seeing Athra made something move in Adriana. She had felt it the last time she was here, but she really didn't know what it was and what it meant. She decided to forget about it for now.

"I'm glad to see you here," Athra confessed. "I was just as concerned about you as I was about Cilicia when I saw you at the hospital."

Athra looked over at the woman she always thought of as a bit more than a friend in moments like these; she saw her more as a little sister. Athra nestled in her egg chair.

Adriana thanked Athra for coming to hospital that day. "I really didn't know who else to call."

Athra skirted around that comment. "How is Cilicia?"

"She's doing better. She is spending some time at my house right now."

"How is that going for everyone?" This was the probing question Athra asked her to get her to reveal those things that were troubling her spirit.

Adriana shared with Athra the events that had led up to Cilicia's attempted suicide, including the fact that Cilicia said she saw Justus masturbating while looking at penises. She decided not to disclose who.

Athra validated Adriana by commending her for helping her friend. Athra could see the burden Adriana was carrying the last time she was there had increased.

"What do you think about her situation with Justus?" Adriana inquired.

"I have worked with couples who were in the same situation. Most women who discover their husband or significant other has been exchanging sex or having sex with other men want to save their marriage or relationship. Ending their marriage or relationship is only an option when other things are present, such as abuse. Most of the women who come in here are trying to save their marriage and reconcile their faith with their reality."

Athra's response alleviated some of the tension in Adriana's spirit. Athra noticed the immediate change in her posture.

Athra could sense Adriana needed some space to process everything in her life. She requested to excuse herself to answer another call.

* * *

Adriana felt relieved to be given permission to stay in her

marriage despite the fact she suspected Gavin was having an affair. She was not ready to let go of what she and Gavin had built; maintaining her sanity and having stability were more important to her than confronting Gavin about his indiscretions.

Her mind would not let go of the thoughts of Gavin being with someone else when he was not with her. Every time he said that his flight took him away from home, she questioned if he was with someone else. She started to view the frustrations he said were due to his job as his guilt for having violated their vows.

The more Gavin tried to engage Adriana, the more she found herself rejecting him. She wanted to be in love with her husband like she had been for almost twenty years; however, something inside of her told her to guard her heart. She wanted to trust him, but she knew how her trust had been taken advantage of in the past.

"No," she said aloud to herself; "you're still not sure how all of this is going to end. What if something else surfaces? Are you willing to take that chance?"

She began to cry. She had never imagined that she would not be the only person giving Gavin love and taking care of his needs. She had never thought that she was not enough for him, that her love would need supplementing to keep him happy.

As she laid restless in her empty bed, her mother came into her room wearing her favorite purple pajamas, the ones Ariadne and Nicklous had given her two Christmases ago. An emerald, green night cap covered the mostly black hair that was a source of Regenia's pride. Adriana was surprised at the visit because her mother only came to her bedroom when she was sick. Seeing her mother began to bring peace to her inharmonious spirit.

Regenia motioned for Adriana to join her in the sitting room once she had entered the space. Adriana slid out of her bed and followed. They rested on the matching chaise lounges that Adriana enjoyed reading in whenever she could secure a quiet moment.

Adriana and Gavin would turn the chairs around and watch the night sky. Occasionally, they would get lucky and witness a meteorite burning in the mesosphere. They liked to point out Mercury and Jupiter, so Adriana decided to focus her attention on finding them while she listened to her mother.

"You are a great mother and wife and just as good of a friend. Cilicia is lucky to have you right now," Regenia began.

Those words surprised Adriana. She began to wonder exactly what her mother was getting at.

"When I left your father, I felt like I was travelling through a bottomless pit. I could not see any light in our marriage; Cilicia is feeling that way now," Regenia carried on with her conversation.

She looked out the window through the trees to the walking path. Then she turned to her daughter.

"You and Gavin have a lot of light in your marriage. He has brought more joy to your life than I could've imagined. I was worried about you before he came into your life. I didn't know if you would find life again when things went awry with Jamie."

Adriana looked over at her mother. Then joined her mother in looking at the path; she was trying to see what her mother was focusing on.

"Justus is not the man Gavin is. He has allowed his desires to control him and put his family in a bad situation. Gavin has continued to grow. It is apparent in that growth that he loves and cares for his family the way a man should."

Regenia looked over at her daughter. "He knows something that your father learned during his second marriage when it was too late for us."

Adriana wondered how that made her mother feel.

"Your stepfather was a man much like Gavin," Regenia said as she smiled returning her gaze from her daughter into the distance. "Maybe watching his first wife die helped him in that way."

Adriana was happy to see her mother's eyes light up. Those lights had become less frequent after her stepfather passed away.

"You and Gavin can get through anything that comes your way. No marriage is successful without something to challenge it, even if it's our own thoughts about a previous marriage."

Adriana read that as the grief her mother felt over her own divorce and her stepfather's grief over his wife's death.

There was silence. Adriana was enjoying the alone time with her mother. It had been a while since they had done this.

Adriana began to cry. She wanted to let her mother know everything that had been bothering her. She wanted to let it all out of her.

"I've been so scared, Mama. I don't want to lose Gavin to anything or anybody. This has really been tough."

"Why do you think I decided to stay? I could see it in you."

Adriana continued to cry in her mother's arms. She was relieved to know that being in her mother's arms felt the same as it did when she was a child.

"Support Cilicia as much as you can, but don't do it at the expense of your own marriage and family. Don't ever think I am not here for you because I have been here for her. You are still the one that IS my heart although she is in my heart," Regenia said to daughter for reassurance.

"I know, Mama," Adriana said. The older she got, the more she understood her mother and appreciated her wisdom. Deep down, she knew that she would never have survived this moment in her life without Regenia being there. She had been the anchor the family needed because her presence brought comfort as they navigated the winds and rains of this hurricane that had developed so quickly in their lives.

Spiritual Guidance

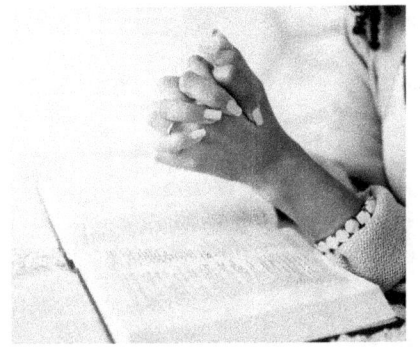

For Women Who Have Attempted Suicide: The Rainbow is More Than Enough *hope*

Choice; we all have a choice;
From one light; the prism separates
To display the beauty of all there is;
God created the rainbow to celebrate diversity;
One person's choice is not always right for another;
But we are still ONE from the same divine light.

The rainbow has to be enough;
It is not going anywhere;
That is what makes it so beautiful;
It comes to us to remind us that
We have a choice.

We can choose what is right for us;
While someone else makes a diverse choice;
It does not mean we are less than or they are more than;
It simply means that we can choose and still be ONE!

faith

17

The 85-15 Support Group

Adriana and Cilicia walked into and looked around the mint green room. They accepted the invitation Athra had extended to join her Wednesday night group. Cilicia observed that none of the ladies were wearing shoes. She called Adriana's name then pointed to an area to her left where shoes had been neatly placed. She and Adriana left their shoes in the same corner and grabbed a pair of fuzzy socks to put on their feet.

Adriana spotted a beverage station that had water infused with fruits and vegetables and hot and cold teas. There was also a snack station with fruits, vegetables, nuts, cheese, hummus, flat bread, and chips. They fixed themselves a snack and stood like the other women in room as they consumed their food.

Athra walked over to the pair. She stood between the two and placed her hand on their backs. "Thanks for coming; we'll begin in about twenty minutes."

Something about Athra's touch made them feel a sense of security.

Adriana looked at her phone as Athra walked away. She had a missed call from Gavin. "I don't want to think about him right now," she thought to herself.

Cilicia looked past the hanging swing chairs to the painting on the wall. She found the lotus flower with the roots that had come out of the water interesting. She had never seen the colors of the rainbow arranged with seven colors instead of six. Feeling a bit confused and lost, she nudged Adriana.

"Is that painting supposed to represent the rainbow or gay pride or something?" Cilicia asked Adriana.

Adriana was a bit surprised by the gay pride analysis. She took a deep breath trying to understand how she might be feeling. "I would say the chakra system because of the seven colors and the fact the colors are above a lotus flower."

Adriana and Cilicia stood silently observing the room's décor, set-up, and the people in the space. Everyone in the room was a woman, and they were wearing socks with the same colors in the lotus rainbow. Just as Adriana and Cilicia finished their snack and water, they heard a chime. The women began to place their glasses and plates on trays then they proceeded to the magenta carpeted area where the hanging swing chairs stood. The bamboo chairs were cushioned with the same colors as the socks and lotus flower.

Athra took a seat in the teardrop shaped chair cushioned with violet, magenta, and white. She crossed her legs then closed her eyes; everyone was silent. It remained that way for a couple of minutes until two people entered the room and took their seats. There were a couple more minutes of silence.

Athra broke the silence with her greeting and disclaimer. "Welcome to 85-15, a spiritual enlightenment group whose mission is to help guide those who attend to a place of peace and tranquility in our lives. Although we have mental health professionals who attend our meetings sometimes, it is not intended to supplant therapy or treatment needed for mental health. We acknowledge that we need them both – mental and spiritual health professionals to help us feel whole because they come together to create excellent emotional health."

She scanned the room for familiar and new faces. She tapped her singing bowl then circled it with the mallet. Adriana and Cilicia noticed that most women took a deep breath then closed their eyes. They did the same.

Adriana's body began to relax even more than it had when she entered the room and smelled frankincense and eucalyptus. She worked hard to center herself and forget about everyone else.

She moved in her seat to find a comfortable position. The silence was bothering her. She couldn't get rid of the guilt for not answering Gavin's call.

Cilicia adjusted herself in her seat. She worked to hold her breath for ten seconds before exhaling. She thought about her husband and her children; she thought about her time in the hospital and the advice given to her by her therapist.

Then Athra tapped her bowl three times; she repeated.

"Who would like to set the stage with a prayer or verse?" Athra requested from the group.

Adriana looked around the circle. Someone wearing yellow raised her hand. Athra nodded her head towards the lady.

The lady, younger than Adriana and Cilicia, began to speak, "'What you see reflects your thinking, and your thinking but reflects the choice of what you want to see.' I read that in *A Course in Miracles*."

Everyone in the room quietly sat as they meditated on the verse.

"That's an interesting verse," someone sitting in a blue chair said to the group.

The lady in yellow responded, "I have been meditating on this verse because I am still coming to terms with the fact that I am sharing my husband. What I want is the traditional marriage that I have seen my parents have, but what I have is a marriage that makes me feel a little less valuable because my husband has been having affairs."

The woman in the blue chair asked if the verse could be reread; the lady in yellow spoke it again.

"Sometimes we want the IMAGE of what our parents portrayed because our scope was limited to what they allowed us to see," the woman in blue responded. "I wanted that image, too, until I had to accept the fact that my father was more homosexual than he was heterosexual. Accepting that my mother married someone who was not my biological father was an eye-opener for me."

"My parents had a good marriage," the lady in yellow said.

"My parents had a good marriage, too. My father was an excellent provider, my parents never argued, my father loved my mother and gave her anything she asked for. That did not change the fact that he was more homosexual than he was heterosexual. It does not change the fact that my mother married him when she was pregnant with me doubting whether I was his child," the woman in blue added.

"It sounds like your mother had an 85-15 marriage," a woman wearing an emerald-colored dress said.

"I believe they did," the lady in blue said. "My mother probably weighed the pros and cons of being married to my father verses marrying my biological father, who was never as financially stable as my father. Rumor has it that she never stopped having an affair with my biological father and that my father always knew."

"Did your mother know the man who raised you was gay?" asked the lady in yellow.

"She probably didn't know at first like the rest of us. As the story goes, he pretty much stopped having sex with her soon after they were married – anniversary trip, Valentine's Day, Mother's Day, Thanksgiving, and Christmas were her days to have sex with him. It makes sense to me when I think about my brother and two sisters being born in April."

Adriana was amazed at how freely the women talked about their lives. She looked at Cilicia. She wondered how much of Cilicia's life had been like the woman in blue's mother.

Athra addressed the lady in yellow. "Catarina, how are you feeling about sharing your husband?"

"Something about my husband having sex with men makes me feel like my marriage isn't secure. But at the same time, I wonder if he will one day leave me because he wants to be with a man," Catarina answered.

"I read that man have sex with other men because they are not having enough sex at home. It doesn't mean they have an emotional attachment with the man, it simply means they are getting physical relief," a woman wearing orange said.

"I don't know what type of connection or attachment he is having," the lady in yellow said. "I really want the type of marriage that is described in the Bible where my husband loves me like Christ loved the church."

"How do you feel about how he loves you?" the woman in green asked.

"I feel like he loves me; that is what is making all of this so hard. He never raises his voice at me, even when I go off on him. If I hit him, he pushes me away," Catarina answered.

"How is your sex life?" the lady in blue asked.

"I don't have a lot of experience with men, but he is the best experience I have ever had. That's another thing I don't understand. I never tell him, 'No'," Catarina shared.

Athra decided to weigh in on the discussion. "Some people are bisexual; that could be the case with your husband, Catarina."

"Does that go against what God wants us to do?" Catarina questioned.

"If we could be in God's mind, then we would not be pondering these things, right?" Athra answered.

Cilicia looked at Athra. She noticed that Sheraton was there, too. She didn't know that Sheraton was going to be there. She thought about the picture she had seen with Sheraton in the background.

"Have you thought about joining your husband on one of his encounters?" Cilicia asked the group.

Catarina answered, "No; that is just something I don't believe in. I believe sex is sacred. The Bible says that marriage is a covenant between husband and wife and God."

Cilicia didn't speak again.

"One thing we have to remember is that men had more than one wife when the Bible was written; our society does not accept that anymore," the woman in blue stated.

"Could this be the reason why so many men are choosing to have sex with other men?" asked the woman wearing orange. "When we think about it, today's societies are much different than societies were back then. Men had many women. I do believe that women back then had lesbian relationships because their husbands were too busy pleasing other women to take care of their needs."

The lady in green commented, "That is why I decided to have a relationship with my best friend. Both of our husbands were truck drivers who were rarely home. We didn't want to let the preacher or deacon take care of our needs, so we took care of each other."

The lady in blue looked at her. "Where is your best friend now?"

"She passed away two years ago. Since she has been gone, I look at our husbands and wonder how close they are. I wonder if they are into each other," the lady in green answered.

Adriana absorbed everything that was being said. A part of her felt relief. If the things Cilicia was saying about Justus and Gavin were true, it didn't mean that she needed to make the decision to leave her husband.

Catarina spoke, "I want to see my husband as a strong man. Does having sex with someone else, especially a man, make him weak?"

The lady in orange spoke, "I have never seen my husband as weak because he has sex with men. In ancient times, men went to war for years. I bet they had sex with each other because there were no women around. No one viewed Alexander the Great or Achilles as weak; history sees them as being strong and heroes."

Another lady in yellow responded, "I never thought about it that way, but I never knew they were gay."

The group sat in tranquility. Athra reached for her bowl to dismiss the group.

Adriana and Cilicia waited to speak to Sheraton before leaving the room. She approached them and introduced them to the lady in orange.

"Shanica, these are my friends Adriana and Cilicia," Sheraton said. "Adriana and Cilicia, Shanica."

"I didn't know you were coming today," Cilicia addressed Sheraton, dismissing her introduction of Shanica.

"We have been coming here for a while," Sheraton said.

"Nice to meet you, Shanica," Adriana said.

Shanica greeted Adriana and Cilicia. "Nice to finally meet you. Sheraton talks about you all the time, especially you, Cilicia."

Wanting to cut the pleasantries short, Sheraton said, "We must leave. I need to get home to the twins." She and Shanica walked away.

Cilicia turned and watched them as they left. "Something about that doesn't feel right."

"I think we need to leave, too," Adriana said heading for the door.

18

Leviticus

    Adriana and Cilicia didn't talk much about the 85-15 Group. However, Cilicia's curiosity about Sheraton and Shanica would come up sometimes. Adriana listened when Cilicia talked about them but kept her thoughts to herself.

    She wondered if Cilicia had made allegations to Sheraton about Winston, or if there was something else going on in the Shelton household.

    As they walked into the room for the second time, they felt more at ease about the group. They knew what to expect. Cilicia searched the room for Shanica, Catarina, and the lady in blue. She was hoping Shanica and Catarina would talk more about their thoughts and feelings. Maybe she could find some understanding of Justus in what the women had to say.

    Cilicia saw the lady in green from last week; she was wearing green again. She waved to her, and the woman waved back.

    Shanica came in wearing an orange blouse and black pants.

"Orange must be her favorite color," Cilicia whispered to Adriana before leaving to greet Shanica.

Cilicia strolled over to the beverage table and greeted Shanica. Cilicia exhaled as she gave Shanica a smile and admired her blouse. "Orange looks really good on you," Cilicia said.

Shanica slightly tilted her head to the left. Cilicia looked at her flawless, hazelnut skin with upturned eyes. Shancia's high cheekbones and full lips made her look like a goddess.

Shanica reached around the back of her neck to gently place her micro braids over her left breast. Then she put most of her weight on her left leg. She extended her right leg. She subtlety licked her lips as she admired the beauty in front of her. She thanked Cilicia for the compliment then raised her glass to take a drink of her pineapple infused water.

Shanicia studied Cilicia, trying to read the woman who was standing in her personal space. Her body language had not given her the response she was looking for. The flattery Cilicia had displayed when she greeted her seemed like bait.

The swift way Cilicia turned then invited Shanica to join her and Adriana left Shanica confused. She accepted the invitation and followed Cilicia to where Adriana was standing.

Adriana was finishing up her cheese and crackers when Cilicia returned with Shanica in tow. Adriana wasn't exactly sure what to make of what Cilicia had done. Over the past week, Cilicia had said more than once something didn't feel right about the situation with Sheraton and Shanica.

Was Cilicia trying to get into Sheraton and Shanica's business? If she was, what good would it do her?

"That's a nice bracelet," Cilicia said, pointing out the silver beaded bracelet on Shanica's right arm with a heart and diamond pendant.

Adriana noticed and complimented Shanica on the bracelet,

too. She watched Cilicia with curiosity. What was she trying to do? Adriana began to feel uneasy about her decision to come. She and Cilicia had made an agreement to share some things with the group but to leave other things for Cilicia's therapist or Athra to deal with in a more private way.

Adriana turned to get more water; Sheraton was standing at the beverage table. She had her right arm crossed over her body; her left elbow was resting in her right hand. She raised the glass she held in her left hand to her lips. Sheraton was squinting her eyes, studying Cilicia and Shanica.

"Nice orange blouse and bracelet," Adriana said, breaking Sheraton's concentration.

Sheraton turned, "Adriana, didn't see you standing there."

"I just walked up," Adriana said. "I needed more water." She refilled her glass then looked at Cilicia and Shanica.

"Cilicia invited your friend to come join us," Adriana said as she returned to the spot where she had left. Sheraton followed her.

Athra gave the three-minute notice that the meeting was about to begin. Sheraton and Shanica sat in the area where they had sat last week; Adriana searched and found a location for her and Cilicia.

Catarina, who wore yellow again, volunteered to give the verse. "'As a loving hind and a graceful doe; Let her breasts satisfy you at all times; Be exhilarated always with her love.' I got that out of Proverbs the fifth chapter and nineteenth verse."

"That is an interesting verse," a woman who was not there last week said.

"I am feeling so confused. If a man is being satisfied by his wife, how can he desire someone else, especially a man? I am trying to decide if I stay married or if I should cut my loses since we don't have any children," Catarina said. "My husband doesn't even know that I saw them. He keeps asking me what's wrong. I just can't bring myself to say the words to him."

"Who says you have to get a divorce?" the woman in blue asked Catarina.

"I live by the Bible, and it says that a man should not lay with a man." Catarina said.

"How would you feel if you found out that most men have some sort of sex with other men?" a woman wearing green, but not the woman from the previous week, asked.

"Does that mean I have to be married to one of them?" Catarina posed the question.

"The odds are higher than most women realize that we have been in a relationship with, had sex with, have been married to, or are married to a man who has had some sort of sexual encounter with another man," said the new woman in green.

Shanica took the opportunity to speak. "My husband is bisexual and so am I."

Well, Adriana thought to herself, Cilicia doesn't need to speculate anymore.

Shancia looked over at Catarina and then the woman in green before going on, "I was relieved when he began to struggle with our sex life. He said that he couldn't keep up with me. I had to be honest with him and let him know that I wanted to be with my roommate again. That's when he told me that he wanted to have the freedom to see his friend. He promised that he would never put anyone before our marriage and that I never needed to worry about another woman. He didn't need to say anything else to me. I got the message."

Adriana was not surprised when Shanica extended her left arm into Sheraton's swing and gently stroked her torso; Sheraton looked over at Shanica with a relaxed body, double blinked her eyes, smiled, then bit her upper lip.

She had listened to Cilicia's rants about something not being right all week long. She wasn't exactly shocked to learn that

Sheraton had a lesbian lover; she had always found her allusive behavior, especially at parties, a bit strange.

There was a time before Winston and Sheraton married when they were at a party. Adriana had gone to the restroom and thought she had seen Sheraton kiss the female bartender. She had never told anyone, not even Cilicia and Gavin, about what she thought she had seen. The woman was not a stranger to Sheraton; she had introduced her to the bartender earlier in the party and said they had attended the same college.

"Do you have a lavender marriage?" someone asked. Adriana missed exactly who the question came from.

"Not really," Shanica answered. "Neither of us want children, which is what attracted us to each other in the first place. We don't want to be tied down."

"It sounds like a lavender marriage to me."

Adriana began to question what exactly the purpose of the 85-15 Group was. Although Athra had always been an understanding and accepting person, she had never shown any signs that would make Adriana question her heterosexuality. Was it for woman who needed to vent because their husbands or partners were having sex with men? Or was it for woman whose husbands were having sex with men, and they met to find a lesbian partner to help them deal with the lack of sex in their marriage?

Could it be that more women were in sexless marriage than Adriana realized? How common was Cilicia's situation. And lavender marriages, Adriana never knew such a thing existed.

Adriana's thoughts were disrupted by Catarina's questions, "Do people in lavender marriages know that is what they have? Is this something that is planned, or something that just happens. I'm so confused."

"I guess it all depends on the couple and the situation," the woman in blue answered.

"The more I come here and listen to what everyone has to say, the more I am accepting that I need to leave my marriage," Catarina said.

"I've already left, and I'm not going back," Cilicia shared with the group. "It's not just that I believe my husband has been having sex with other men, he is abusive to me, too." Cilicia's confession allowed others to share their stories.

Catarina began to speak, "For years my husband has been punishing me for having a mind of my own by withholding sex from me. If I say something or do something he does not like, there is no sex for a month or two. I'm not a child; I don't need him to be my daddy. When I saw him having sex with one of our neighbor's husbands, I understood why it was okay for him to go months without sex. He didn't want to be with me anyway. Now, I'm beginning to understand that my husband is very abusive – emotionally and psychologically."

A woman wearing violet shared her story. "I stay in my marriage for financial reasons. My husband told me after the birth of our second child that he had done his duty. He moved out of our bedroom before our son was three months old. Then he accepted a job that takes him out of town two to four months at a time. He comes home about one week a month, and the children and I visit him when he can't come to us. I finally decided to get a lover, which helps a little. I am still lonely and would love to have the man I married back in my bed."

Cilicia spoke; "My husband has been withholding sex from me for four years. At first, he said it was because I had gained so much weight since we got married. I didn't complain about him gaining weight since our marriage; I guess he wasn't looking in the mirror. So, I joined Weight Watchers, went to the gym, and lost over thirty pounds all while he gained a few more pounds. We had sex about five times that year. Then he said I had stopped fixing myself up, so I spent money we couldn't afford on more expensive clothes and shoes. I went to the spa to get wax jobs and the salon for nails and lashes. Then he said it was my spending habits that were the reasons why he wasn't attracted to me. Can you imagine having sex seven times in the past six years?"

Athra broke the silence, "Research says that most women do not leave their marriages because their husbands are having sex with men. Women whose husbands are having sex with men leave because of abuse or some other issues in the marriage."

Adriana understood what Athra was saying. Despite what Cilicia had been saying over the past few months, there was almost nothing in Adriana's marriage that made her want to leave Gavin. The discovery of the other cell phones might have a big toe out the door.

Adriana thought about the advice Maurice gave her a few days before her wedding. "Sometimes a man needs to get his feet wet. It doesn't mean he has forgotten his wife. You might need to get your feet wet, too. Just remember to go to the beach with someone who is married and don't stay at the same place too long. That's when things get complicated."

Had Gavin been given the same advice by his father? Was that why he went to Blair instead of someone else? Did he have a phone for each lover?

Adriana's mind was plagued with many things, even her love for Gavin.

Adriana pulled her leg into the swing and rested her head on the back of her chair. She considered everything she had heard and was listening to for the rest of the meeting.

A woman wearing a navy, blue dress began to speak. "I had a woman from my church to befriend me so that she could spend more time with my husband. I enjoyed our friendship; we even took vacations with our husbands and went on martial retreats together. Little did I know they were all ways for her to spend more time with my husband. When her husband found out about their affair, he told me about my frenemy. He said that his wife was into anal sex, and he wasn't, so she found someone who would give her what she wanted. He found out about the affair because his wife had videos on her phone of them having sex. Can you imagine that? He watched her unlock her phone until he memorized the code then found them. He showed me a couple of the videos. He's getting a divorce on the grounds of adultery. I'm still trying to decide what I want to do about my marriage. My husband is a deacon in the church, so leaving him won't be easy."

The woman in green asked, "Was the issue in your marriage you wouldn't have anal sex with him?"

The woman in navy blue answered, "Even if I would've had anal sex with him, he would've still cheated with her. She was not his first time cheating. It's just that her husband is the first person to confront him and let me know."

Listening to the woman in navy blue's story, Adriana had her question answered. This was a group of women whose husbands were having affairs in general, and they were trying to hold on to their marriages.

"Marital betrayal happens in all areas of our lives," Athra said. "What we must do is examine ourselves to answer the question, 'How does this make me feel?' If we are in a situation that makes us feel unsafe, devalued, less than who God created us to be, then we must make some decisions on how we are going to resolve those feelings."

She continued, "We all continue to grow in many areas of our lives - even after marriage. For some of us, we find or rediscover things about ourselves that have been suppressed and need to be expressed to regain our sense of self. It is not uncommon for this to happen once we are married because most of us are in our twenties when we make that commitment."

Everyone had their attention focused on Athra, "We marry because we believe we are in love and/or we feel we are in a good place in our lives to take the next step in our process of growth, which societies tell us is marriage and parenthood. All the while we are still trying to reconcile who we actually are with society's expectations of who we should be based on our gender.

"Very seldom do we realize that we are still on the path and growth of self-discovery once we are married. Some of the things that lie within us we may not begin to recognize until we are out of the identity of our parents and in the safety and security of a marriage. Why? Because this is the person who has vowed to love and accept us for who we really are. This is the person we no longer must wear a mask for. This is the person we share our most intimate and personal space with for decades on end. When we begin to let our guards down within ourselves, then ourselves are revealed to us. If we don't like what we see, we begin to fight against those things because our cultures, religions, and society tell us that is not how things are supposed to be."

Athra paused and looked around the room.

"Thirty is a critical age in human development because we gain more understanding of ourselves and the world around us. Those things that are in us, that society tells us are religiously and morally wrong, we try to fight against. Sometimes we take that fight outside of ourselves to the ones we love – our spouses and children. They are the closest and most accessible to us; they are in our secret and safe space - our homes.

"The problem people are trying to solve is that which is on the inside and that which is expected of us on the outside. This vicious cycle has lasted for eons. I have no doubt that when Moses included that man shall not lie with men in Leviticus, it was because he was establishing a society that was unique from others – a god that cannot be seen or represented in an image; an all-knowing, universal god; and the forbidding a sexual practice that was common in Egypt and Sumer, Abraham's place of origin.

"Abrahamic religions are the dominant religions in today's world. Whereas other societies or civilizations did not look down upon same-sex relationships between men based on social status, Abrahamic societies appeared to totally condemn them. Where does that leave us today? With men who have certain desires fulfilling those desires in ways that keep them out of society's sight, which is why we are here."

Athra paused. She looked around the circle. No one spoke.

"The challenge that we all face, which is another reason why we are here, is how do we reconcile within ourselves," Athra held her clasps hands to her heart, "that which we know is right for a person with what society expects. Sexuality is not as cut and dry as society teaches us to think it is. Sexuality in humans is on a gray scale. The Kinsey Scale was developed to help today's people understand sexual orientation."

Adriana noticed that everyone, including herself, had relaxed in their seats.

"Men having sex with men, even those who were married, was not as taboo throughout human history as we have been taught to think. How do we know? Manuscripts and drawings from before the common era and within the common era speak of those societal norms. Going back to the book of Leviticus, it is the book that contained the principles and laws for the Hebrews to live by. What could be another reason why the law forbids a man to lay with another man as a man lays with a woman? Could it be that the Hebrews, who had left Egypt and were establishing themselves as a nation, needed to repopulate themselves to be able to develop their identity?

"Do we know how many men or boys could have lost their lives trying to flee Egypt or while in the desert eating manna?

Men would be needed to withstand established nations, such as the Egyptians, Nubian, Hitties, and Amorites. Moses knew that he needed hundreds of thousands of men to defend the Hebrews against all the other nations and civilizations that had already been established since before Abraham answered God's call to leave Ur. Moses knew he had to establish an identity for Abraham's descendants apart from the identity that incorporated Egyptian culture and customs. The Hebrew needed men placing their seed in as many women as possible to multiply as quickly as possible to establish that new identity, which could only be achieved by men not having sexual relations with men."

Athra, who had been sitting at the edge of her seat as she spoke to the group, sat back and relaxed in her chair. "Keep in mind. Every commandment we read in the Bible instructs the Hebrew people to multiply, even when there were people already in the world."

The room remained silent for a couple of minutes.

Curled up in a chair directly across from Adriana was a young woman wearing red. She was there last week in the same position with the same light gold throw draped over her body. "What about the fact that today's men having sex with men is why women are getting infected with HIV? Isn't that why God created HIV in the first place, to stop men from having sex with men? God wanted men to stop having sex with men because the law in the Bible says it is an abomination," was uttered from the face whose eyes had a blank stare, as if it had disconnected from the world entirely.

The woman in navy blue, who Adriana later learned was a pharmacist spoke, "HIV has not been around that long. It was in the 1980's when we started talking about AIDS and HIV. We know that HIV and AIDS were not around when Moses wrote the laws. Human sexuality is much older than any virus or disease we have today."

The woman in navy blue continued, "That's why groups like this are important. We must help ourselves by facing the fact that our husbands are struggling just as much as we are. We need to drop little hints to them, encouraging them to use protection if they are going to have sex with other people – man or woman. And if we choose to have sex with other people, we need to do the same."

The group sat silent for a few minutes. Then Athra tapped her bowl and circled her mallet around it. She stood, and the women in the circle did the same. She reached out her hands and the women next to her locked their hands into hers. The women in the group bowed their heads.

"God, our great creator of all there is here in your great kingdom we call Earth, we lift you up and praise you for the opportunity to do your will. We embrace all our sisters here today because her life is ours. We know you to be a great healer; a redeemer; and a way maker, so we beseech you today to heal our hearts; minds; and spirits as we grow through and go through this phase of our lives. Continue to lead us and guide us to the place of peace we are seeking in this moment. When we return to our homes, send your angels before us, clearing the path so that we can know what your will is for our lives. Strengthen us to accept what is revealed as truth and guide us to the solution that has already been ordained by you. Allow us to forgive ourselves for those things we need forgiveness for. Allow us to forgive others we feel have trespassed against us. Allow us to exhibit love and understanding to ourselves and others. In all things we honor you; we praise you; and we know that all things work out for the goodness of our lives. So, it is and so it shall be now and forevermore. AMEN."

Adriana and Cilicia skipped to the parking lot amidst the trickling rain. Adriana appreciated the coldness of the rain so much that she didn't bother to remove her coat before starting her car.

The woman in red sparked curiosity and sympathy in Adriana

and Cilicia. Cilicia recalled a radio show was had listened to many years ago.

"The woman was feeling lost because she had test positive for HIV. She said that her husband was the only person she had ever been with. They were high school sweethearts and both virgins. She couldn't understand how she could've contracted the virus when her husband kept saying he had been faithful. Her husband refused to get himself test…. He probably knew he was positive even before she got tested."

"That's such a said story," Adriana said. "It does make me wonder about Red."

Cilicia disclosed to Adriana, "I took an HIV test when I went for my pap smear. It was negative."

"Mine was negative, too," Adriana said.

19

Confession

Cilicia could not convince Adriana to go to the apartment with her. She had made an appointment with an attorney to begin divorce proceedings. She wanted Justus out of the house before she and the children returned, but he was refusing to leave. She never disclosed to him that she had a key to the apartment; she needed leverage in court and not in her battle at home.

She was relieved the locks had not been changed. She pushed open the door. She was stunned the lights were on. She walked into the living room. Clothes were sprawled on the back of the couch. Her heart began to pound. At first glance, at least one set of clothing belonged to a woman. She looked over and saw Sheraton and Shanica.

"What the..." she yelled.

Sheraton and Shanica, who were lying on their sides, looked towards the voice. They jumped when they saw Cilicia.

"Sheraton?" Cilicia said with disappointment in her voice. "Don't tell me that you come here to swing, too." Cilicia had her face contorted as if she was disgusted.

"I don't think my private life is your business," Sheraton said.

"When I told you that Justus was masturbating with naked pictures of Winston, when I told you that I found pictures of him swinging, when I told you about this apartment, you knew the whole time what was going on," Cilicia said.

The sadness in her voice and eyes that were beginning to disconnect began to make Sheraton feel guilty. By the time Sheraton began to speak again, she had wrapped herself in the blanket. Shanica retreated to the bedroom with their clothes.

"It's not my place to get involved in your marriage, Cilicia. That's between you and Justus," Sheraton gently said.

"But you knew about this place, and you knew what he had been doing. When I came to you about my suspicions and when I gave you evidence, you could've said something to me," Cilicia argued.

Sheraton didn't want to get into an argument with Cilicia; however, she could not forget how fragile she still was. She grabbed her phone and texted Adriana to come to the apartment. She was afraid of how all of this would work out.

"I know what I do," Sheraton pointed out, placing her hand on her chest. "I can't speak to you about what anyone else does."

"Does Winston know about you and Shanica?"

"Yes," Sheraton answered bracing herself for the next question.

"Did you know about Justus and Winston before I showed you the pictures he had on his phone?"

Sheraton remained silent.

"WELL! Did you or not?" Cilicia began to yell. "ALL OF THIS TIME, I'VE BEEN GOING CRAZY. AND YOU WERE ONE OF THE ONES GETTING DOWN WITH THEM!"

Cilicia raised her hands to her head. "Don't tell me Adriana is in on it too."

Sheraton felt the urgent need to calm Cilicia's storm. "She has never been here. She doesn't even know about this place."

"She does now," Cilicia said. "How could you do this to me?"

"I haven't done anything to you. I'm just living my life."

"Fucking another woman?" Cilicia asked as she extended her arms to the area where Sheraton and Shanicia had been lying?

"Yes; fucking another woman. That's what bisexual women do," Sheraton said, feeling the need to defend herself.

Shanica walked out of the room. Sheraton looked at her with frustration. "Could you at least put some clothes one?"

"Maybe she wants to join us," Shanica said walking towards Cilicia.

Sheraton looked at her. She tilted her head. "Really, Shanica. I can't believe you right now. She's not into women; I told you that already."

"How would she know if she's never tried it?" Shanica asked.

Sheraton was getting frustrated with her lover. "You know what," she said as she walked towards the room, "I'm not doing this with you tonight."

She rushed into the room to put her clothes on. "Cilicia, I'll be right out."

Sheraton was out of the room in less than a minute. "I'll be back," she said to Shanica. "Come on; let's go," she addressed Cilicia.

Sheraton walked Cilicia to the apartment's lobby. She waited quietly for Adriana to arrive. Sheraton refused to explain to Adriana what had happened. She told her they would have to talk later.

* * *

Athra was sitting behind her desk when Adriana walked in. She had prepared herself for the visitors who followed Adriana into her office.

Athra used her feet to push away from her desk, then swirled her chair to the left. She gently lifted herself from her sitting position to greet the trio.

She had purposefully chosen the purple, wide legged jumpsuit made from bamboo fabric for this session. She had added a pearl belt to give her strength to approach one of the most challenging parts of her ministry – betrayal whether it be between a wife and her husband or long-time friends.

Adriana had given her a detailed background as to why they needed to do this outside of the group. Athra also knew that Cilicia had not recovered from her hospitalization. She understood that for Adriana to move forward in her life, she would have to resolve the issues in her relationship with Cilicia.

"Welcome, ladies," Athra greeted the women. She extended her hand to Cilicia then to Sheraton. Adriana was already heading to the lounge area as Athra was doing her greeting.

Adriana noticed there were three lounge chairs instead of one. She took the middle chair. Adriana immediately noticed the music playing in the background. She had heard music in the waiting room; however, Athra had never played music in their sessions.

Athra smiled at the friends sitting in front of her. She leaned back in her chair then placed her right knee over her left knee. She took a deep breath.

Cilicia closed her eyes then took a deep breath, too.

Athra closed her eyes and took another deep breath. She used her inhalation to sense the energy between the friends. She repeated it three more times.

Sheraton and Adriana joined Athra and Cilicia in their breathing exercises.

Cilicia shifted in her seat. She struggled to keep up the breathing. She couldn't relax the way she had been able to in the group. The music coming through the surround sound speakers was starting to get to her head.

CONFUSION, COMPASSION, CONFESSION - 167

In less than three minutes, everyone except for Athra had opened their eyes. It was clear that being in the present moment was difficult for the friends.

They watched as Athra continued her breathing for a couple more minutes. They watched as she pushed her abdomen out on her inhalations then drew it in on her exhalations. It all seemed to come so naturally to her.

"Don't worry," Athra began to address the group, "you will do better the next time."

"How did you know our eyes were opened?" Sheraton questioned.

Adriana and Cilicia turned to her in amazement. She was usually the shy, most apprehensive one in the group.

"I could feel it," Athra answered.

There was no response from anyone. Silence remained for the next ninety seconds, which seemed almost like an eternity.

"It is so nice to see the friendship among you," Athra openly observed to ease into the session. "How long have you been friends?"

"Cilicia and I were roommates in our freshman year of college until she met Justus our second semester and fell in love," Adriana answered.

Adriana waited for Cilicia to answer how Sheraton became a friend; she never did. She leaned over and looked over at Sheraton to answer.

"Our husbands are partners in an accounting firm," Sheraton answered, pointing between herself and Cilicia.

"All three of our husbands are real estate partners. They have a rental company," Sheraton finished her explanation.

"Impressive, so you have been friends for a very long time," Athra added.

"Yeah," Sheraton said looking at her friends.

"What brings us here today?" Athra looked to the trio for an answer.

Adriana took a hard swallow as she looked from one friend to the other. "Cilicia," she said.

Cilicia looked at her with a mixture of disappointment and anger.

"Our husbands have been swinging and having sex with each other," Cilicia answered.

Athra looked straight at the group. She observed Sheraton as she sank her body into her chair. It was as if she wanted to melt into the furniture and become one with it.

Adriana relaxed her body in her chair. She tilted her head back and closed her eyes. Athra observed her as a tear seemed to form in the inside corner of her right eye.

Athra focused her attention on Cilicia, who was not relaxing in her chair but sitting on the edge of it. She had taken off her shoes and was bending over with her knees touching her chest. She began to rock back and forth.

"Adriana invited us to come see you outside of the group because she believes we could use more spiritual guidance as we work through leaving our husbands," Cilicia announced.

Athra worked hard to maintain her composure; she was unaware that Adriana had made that decision.

"Do you think individual sessions would work better for you?" Athra asked the question more to Cilicia than to Adriana and Sheraton.

"I am the only one of us who can say what is truly the problem in our marriage. Adriana and Sheraton want to act as if our husbands swinging and having sex with each other is not an issue for them," Cilicia answered.

Then she looked at Sheraton. "I stand corrected. SHE has already been swinging with her husband. She even has a girlfriend."

"Adriana and Sheraton, is that how you see it?" Athra wanted to know.

Adriana took the opportunity to speak.

"We don't know if our husbands are having sex with each other or not. We have seen a couple of videos that made it seem like they were at a sex party," she said.

"Really, Adriana," Cilicia confronted her friend. "I told you that Justus had a naked picture of Gavin on his phone. I showed you a video of your friend Blair where there was a threesome with Justus and Gavin. You mean to tell me that you don't believe they are having sex with each other?"

The threesome video was new to Adriana. She felt so embarrassed; she wanted to bleed into her chair. She began to hate Cilicia. How could she keep doing this to her?

Athra studied the expression on Adriana's face. "Cilicia," she held out her hand towards her, "I think you need to let Adriana have some space here."

Cilicia dropped her arms from around her knees. She lowered her legs, then fell back on her chair.

"Gavin and Winston are not Justus," Adriana declared. Then she looked at Athra.

"Gavin and Winston are not Justus," Adriana felt the need to repeat the fact to Cilicia. "Our marriages are not Cilicia's marriage," she looked at Athra. She was searching for a signal as to how far she should go.

"Are you here because you are seeking answers about getting a divorce, or are you here because you feel your friendship is being threatened?" Athra solicited.

"Cilicia seems to think that we should leave our husbands because she needs to leave hers," Sheraton said. "She's been to the 85-15 Group; she knows that some people are okay being in their marriage just the way it is."

"Really," Cilicia said as she sat up. "I knew something was skeptical about you and that girl.

"Our husbands are screwing each other. I have seen at least two videos of them at an orgy. It looks like they are getting down with whoever is in the room, including each other. Are you sure they haven't been getting down with you, too?" Cilicia leaned forward to look at Sheraton.

"I've never been intimate with your husbands," Sheraton defended herself.

"I don't know why I'm here," Adriana finally answered. "I thought I was here to help my friend, but I don't know anymore."

Adriana paused.

"I must admit. Cilicia has been testing our friendship with these shenanigans. We made a promise to never do this to each other. I don't want to keep going on like this."

"Okay," Athra nodded. "Adriana has given her answer."

"Cilicia is pushing boundaries that have nothing to do with her. Adriana and I don't have the same issues in our marriage that she has in hers," Sheraton said.

"Cilicia, how do you feel about what Adriana and Sheraton have said?" Athra questioned.

"Does it not say in the Bible that having sex with a man is an abomination towards the Lord?" Cilicia asked.

"So, are you saying that you are here questioning what the Bible says about getting a divorce?" Athra asked.

"I know what the Bible says," Cilicia answered with subtle anger. "Friends shouldn't betray friends, and women should not stay in a marriage with a man who prefers men over her."

Athra looked at Cilicia. "You have clearly made your decision to divorce your husband. It seems that Adriana and Sheraton have clearly made their decision to stay."

"Why, Adriana would you even consider staying in a marriage to someone who is having sex with another man. Isn't that the reason you broke up with Jamie?" Cilicia asked.

Adriana looked at Cilicia. "I'm not discussing my marriage with you. You have been staying in my home; you can see that Gavin and I don't have the same issues you are experiencing with Justus," Adriana said before she paused.

"Every time you and Justus had a fight, I listened to you. I never told you that you should leave him. I never involved myself in your marriage."

Athra observed a bit of anger rise in Adriana. She had never witnessed that side of her.

"What are you trying to say?" Cilicia asked Adriana. It was apparent she was confronting her.

Adriana's countenance changed. Athra lifted her remote to turn on the music again.

"Okay, ladies," Athra said. "Let's take a moment to stretch."

Athra led the trio into a standing position.

"Let's stand on our tiptoes and reach for the heavens with our fingertips," Athra instructed as she modeled.

"Let's hold this position for a moment."

Athra could feel her anxiety level begin to rise. Adriana requested this session with her friends because she feared what Cilicia would do to herself again. She was trying her best to keep the anxiety down in the room.

Athra lowered her arms and stood flat on her feet.

"Let us inhale the scent of lavender to help us relax," she instructed, leading the trio into taking deep cleansing breaths.

Adriana and Sheraton followed along. Cilicia resisted what was being offered to her.

"We are safe here," Athra said in a calming voice that had a little more bass than usual; she looked directly at Cilicia. "We have no reason to fear anything, especially our friends. We are safe."

She led the trio into a downward dog pose; they mimicked the pose.

"We are safe in our own decisions," she continued. "God and the universe have created a safe place for us to be. Everyone is safe here."

She led the trio to a standing position. Then she sat down. The trio followed her lead.

"Ladies, please close your eyes and listen to the music for a couple of minutes. No talking until I return," Athra instructed.

In less than a minute she had returned with four cups of ice cream.

"I'm not worrying about the pounds right now," she said as she distributed the treat.

The friends accepted the vanilla ice cream without a fuss.

Athra returned to her seat then began eating her ice cream.

"True friendship has a lot of the same characteristics as one might see in a marital relationship," Athra began.

"We can feel rejection when our friends disagree with us just as we might feel rejection if our spouse does not agree with us. However, we cannot let a difference of opinions or diversity in the way we choose to live our lives threaten something so precious as the bond that has been created over decades," Athra said.

The tension that was in the room fifteen minutes ago had begun to ease.

"I understand why Cilicia has decided to divorce Justus," Sheraton said. "It's not just the sex thing that has given her a reason to leave. There are many things going on in her marriage that are not in mine or Adriana's. I respect the decision she had made for herself and her children."

"Do we all understand that?" Athra inquired.

Cilicia lowered her cup and spoon. She placed them between her legs. Tears flowed.

Sheraton began to move from her chair. Athra pushed her left hand out. Sheraton slid back on her seat.

"Cilicia, can you tell us how you're feeling?" Athra asked.

"I love Justus," Cilicia said. "I truly love him. I have known for years that I need to leave him. I don't know how to move forward in a world that does not include him."

"What do you not know?" Athra questioned.

"I don't know how to make a life that does not include him. I don't know what God will say to me on judgment day about me breaking my up family," Cilicia answered.

"Why have you decided to divorce him?" Athra questioned.

"Because he has an apartment with his friends where they have sex parties. Because he is having sex with men," Cilicia answered.

"Sex with men is a dealbreaker for you?" Athra probed.

"I think that is the thing that has made me realize that nothing in my marriage will get better," Cilicia divulged.

Silence.

"Justus does not love me the way I love him," Cilicia acknowledged.

"Is there anything that can happen to repair your marriage?" Athra challenged Cilicia to ponder.

"I have already done everything that I can do to keep our marriage together. It seems that he had done everything to tear it apart," Cilicia admitted.

Athra looked at her arm. She had been alerted by her receptionist that the next client would be arriving in less than fifteen minutes.

"I would like to see each of you again individually," Athra announced. "We can still work together in this small group and in the 85-15 Group; however, I think we need to focus on some individual things that would help strengthen the friendship."

"I am not ready to leave right now," Cilicia said. She looked up at Athra pleading for help.

"Adriana, how do you feel about leaving with Sheraton while I spend more time with Cilicia?" Athra asked.

"We are okay leaving," Adriana said, answering for herself and Sheraton. Cilicia was more than they could handle together, and Adriana needed the break. Cilicia had been crowding her space. She needed time to process her own feelings about what Cilicia had just said. It seemed that her life was snowballing out of control.

Adriana and Sheraton left the room.

Athra sent a message to her receptionist instructing her to let the next person know she would be with him shortly.

20

The Hummingbird

Athra gave Cilicia a box of tissues. She excused herself from the room to give her a little time to herself. A lot had happened when the trio was there, and Cilicia had a lot riding on her shoulders.

"I am going to see Mr. Evers. Give Cilicia about five minutes then carry her a journal. Instruct her to write how she is feeling. I will return shortly," Athra instructed her assistant as she went into the room to see Mr. Evers.

Athra whispered a prayer before entering the room. Mr. Evers, who was working through his own identity issues, was trying to hold on to the image he had created in his younger years that was beginning to crack. His recent sobriety led to a spiritual awakening and the desire to release things from his past. He had chosen Athra as the person to guide him through his transformation.

* * *

Athra returned to Cilicia sleeping in a fetal position. She returned to her chair then swirled to look out the window. She focused on the garden area designed to attract hummingbirds.

She looked at the bird splash with a feeder in the middle. There was no sign of a hummingbird. Then she diverted her eyes to the feeder that hung from a stake just a few feet from the splash. Still not luck. She rose from her chair then walked to the window. She stood close to the window to look at her lilies. There among the Asiatic lilies she saw wings flapping. She focused her attention on the little wonder that was maintaining its position and composure while still doing what it needed to do to feed itself.

Athra watched the bird as it moved from one lily to the other. She allowed her mind to go blank. She simply observed the creature that seemed to have no worries in the world. Then she put her hands in her pockets.

"Everything that you do, you begin to think you are," she said to herself.

Cilicia cleared her throat. Athra was unaware she was awake.

"How do you feel?" Athra asked.

"Like I've been hit by a bullet train," Cilicia answered.

"That bad?"

"Worse."

Athra moved away from the window to approach Cilicia.

"I never pray for anyone unless I am given permission to do so," she said to Cilicia.

"I thought you were a minister; someone who leads people to a higher place, or whatever Adriana said about you," Cilicia said.

"I am, and I am, and I am," Athra answered. "I take the universal spiritual law of healing very seriously."

"The what?"

"The universal spiritual law of healing. One thing we must understand on our spiritual path is that we must respect a person's decisions about her life," Athra informed.

"Okay," Cilicia said.

"I do not want to pray for anything about your life until you are clear about what you desire. What do you know about yourself, Justus, and your marriage?"

"I know that my marriage is over and has been for a long time."

"Okay. Is your marriage something that can be healed?"

"My husband does not want it to get better. He told me during our last encounter that he has been trying to get me to cheat on him so he could get custody of our children."

The admission was not something Athra was expecting to hear. She had known men who tried to get their wives to have affairs to minimize their financial impact should a divorce happen but one who admitted to trying to gain custody was a new one.

Athra shook her head. "It is still all the same. If he gets custody, he minimizes his financial impact and may even gain," she thought to herself.

"Are you saying that he has decided to end the marriage?" Athra inquired for a deeper understanding.

"He has decided that he does not want our marriage. We have not slept in the same bed in over two years. We have not had sex in over four. Before then I had to make appointments and let him know in advance that I wanted sex," Cilicia admitted.

"The issues you raised earlier are valid," Athra acknowledged.

"The last time I caught him jacking off while looking at Gavin's picture was not the first time. I caught him looking at gay porn on his phone about four months ago. I think that's when I knew it was over. He doesn't want me; he wants men," Cilicia said with tears in her voice.

"Is that what makes you believe your marriage is over?" Athra questioned.

"It is physical abuse, drug use, and issues with money, too. It's everything," Cilicia shared. She looked as if all life had left her.

"Cilicia," Athra began. "I am a divorced woman. There comes a time when we must make a decision that is right, not just for ourselves, but also for our children. No one can tell us when that time comes. For some it never comes. For others it comes in the first seven years of their marriage. For others it comes much later."

"Are you saying the time has come for me to leave my husband?"

"I am saying the time has come for you to search yourself to know the answer to that question. Searching yourself means that you must create a deeper connection with God," Athra said.

"How do I know when I have received the answer?" Cilicia asked.

"How do you know you have not received the answer?" Athra countered.

Cilicia lowered her eyes. She pulled the string that was hanging from her hem.

"It came before I saw him the last time," Cilicia whispered. "I was just hoping it would be something else."

The women sat in silence. The sound of a waterfall was helping to create calm in the room.

"When did it come for you?" Cilicia asked.

"I can say that it came to me one night when God spoke to my spirit and said, 'I put everything you need in you.' It still took me a few months to find it in me to accept that I would have to make a life for myself and my daughter," Athra shared.

"Were you a minster before or after your divorce?" Cilicia questioned.

"Both," Athra answered rising from her seat. She walked to her desk then sat on the edge.

"I always knew in my heart that I would someday become a minister. I just didn't know how. I underwent quite a bit of spiritual growth before I was able to leave my first husband. It was not an easy decision to leave the marriage that I thought had given me all I had prayed to God for," Athra shared.

"I had to accept that it was a toxic situation that would determine how my daughter would live her life and how she would view marriage. I did not want her to think that abuse is normal in a relationship."

Athra continued to listen.

"My dad cheated on my mom when we were growing up. I remember listening to my father hitting my mother when she tried to encourage him to focus on his ministry instead of temptations that took him away from God. He would go through cycles of drinking sometimes. He eventually stopped drinking and hitting my mom," Cilicia shared.

"Every night, I prayed that he would stop hitting my mom. I didn't go back home after my sophomore year of college because I felt powerless over what was happening, and I was tired of keeping secrets. I knew my mother would never leave, so I went to summer sessions and found summer jobs to stay in Greensboro."

"Some people do change, but it takes a lot of work on their part," Athra said.

"It was the wreck he had that killed the son he had with a woman before he married my mother that changed him. He was already a preacher when my brother got killed. He didn't do it because he got some divine inspiration," Cilicia said.

"Who is to say the wreck was not the divine inspiration?"

"I never thought about it. I guess seeing my brother's body helped him realize how dangerous his addiction was. Looking at my brother's body gave him a sense of his own mortality.

"He used to say that the devil didn't let him go until he became a preacher. If the devil had him before he became a preacher, I would've hated to see what he was like before that time. I know what type of hell I lived in," Cilicia said.

Deep contemplation proceeded Athra's response. "Addictions are not easy to overcome. It takes us facing those parts of ourselves that bring us pain, that keeps people in their cycles of usage.

"One of the Twelve Steps of Alcoholics Anonymous requires a

person to take moral inventories. Within our moral inventory of our past actions lies the clue to our pain.

"Now, another step is looking at our character defects. Most character defects develop from our attempts to manage childhood trauma. That is why the next step has people soliciting God to remove our shortcomings. Because we have all sinned and fallen short of God's glory."

"He was never as bad as Justus is," Cilicia said.

"He didn't have to be to need to work through the twelve steps," Athra replied.

The women went silent. Cilicia turned to look out the picture window. A hummingbird had just landed on the birdbath. It used its beak to flip water onto its back.

"God answers our questions in some of the most mysterious of ways," Athra said as she, too, watched the bird take its bath.

A hundred yards away stood one of the original elms trees the garden was designed around. A few yards away from it was a pecan tree. Sunlight was making its way through the majestic leaves and casting shadows on the grass that was cut high.

"Since you already have your shoes off, let's take a walk," Athra said.

She led Cilicia through the door to the left of the window. Athra stopped at the outdoor storage container and retrieved a bundle. Then she opened the refrigerator to get a bottle of water.

The ladies began their journey through the garden.

Cilicia noticed how the grass felt more like carpet than grass.

"My first husband used to cut our grass high," Athra said, admiring the splendor of the scene. The grass is cut high to help me remember the goodness that lies in everything and everybody."

"How did you know I was thinking about the grass?" Cilicia asked.

"Most people have questions about the grass," Athra answered.

They walked slowly past the lilies as the morning sun beamed down on them. Then they approached the birdbath. The grass near the birdbath had more warmth than the grass near the lilies.

"Every year we have a Fall Festival. Young children and elders pick and shell pecans," Athra shared. "The nuts are medium brown with just the right amount of butter and sweetness to them. I usually save some as a topping for my ice cream."

By the time they reached their destination, the shade from the trees had kept the grass cool and still protected the dew embedded near the soil.

Athra unrolled the bundle that was placed under her arm.

"You have about an hour before lunchtime," Athra told her. "We usually have two to four guests who come to this garden during their lunch."

Cilicia turned to get a view of the garden. She saw two swings, another hammock stand, and three benches.

"Sometimes we need space, alone time with God," Athra said.

Athra had finished hooking the hammock to its stand. "I wanted you to see the options you have for this space. Sometimes people choose to sit on the grass."

Cilicia began to understand what Athra was trying to do for her. She accepted the bottle of water being offered to her.

"We hope you find some usage in this sanctuary," Athra said. "I will be right there," she pointed to the picture window, "when you are ready."

Cilicia looked at the window that looked more like a mirror from the outside.

"Now, about that prayer," Athra said.

Cilicia nodded her head in agreement.

Athra faced Cilicia and held both of her hands in her hands.

"God, we come to you today expressing our gratitude for your presence in our lives. We thank you for this beautiful morning and opportunity to experience this wonderful life in this magnificent creation we have named Earth. We open ourselves to allow the Holy Spirit to touch us, to open our minds to receive clear and peaceful answers to the questions that we are seeking answers to. We allow the Holy Spirit to guide us into the acceptance of those answers with peace and courage to live through what has been revealed to us. We accept your word and will for our lives and allow them to become the armor that will protect us and defend us as we transition our lives and those we love into your will. We allow the Holy Spirit to lead us along the path and clear the way for our growth and attainment. We allow the Holy Spirit to give us discernment and foresight to learn the forces and powers that are for our good and the good of those we love. We allow the Holy Spirit to cover us, our descendants, and all who are connected to us in your mercy and grace now and forevermore. So, it shall be and so it is. AMEN!"

Athra released Cilicia's hands then turned to walk back to the building.

21

Matthew 19:12

The 85-15 Support Group's third meeting of the month is dedicated to reading letters from anonymous writers. Carlyse, Athra's assistant, read the letters to the group. The writers selected a color from the chakra spectrum to represent themselves as a member of the group. Each woman who sat in the circle chose her seat based on how she was feeling for that day.

Carlyse read the first letter:

Dear Athra and Group,

I have been married for over four years. When I met my husband, I had turned my life over to God, so we didn't have sex until after we got married. I have tried my best to make the marriage work, but I am miserable. My husband's penis is too big for me. I don't like having sex with him, but I do it anyway. I recently gave in to the temptations of my daughter's daddy because his size is more comfortable and pleasurable. He has changed a lot since we broke up, and he thinks we should give our relationship another chance. I have another daughter with my husband. My husband has always been more responsible than my older daughter's father. I am trying my best to focus on all the good in our marriage, but the sex part overwhelms every time I am with my husband. I am miserable!! Should I give my older daughter's father a second chance, or should I accept the 80-20 and stay with my husband?

Signed, Green

Chandra, the women in navy blue, was the first person to address the letter. "I've always heard of women complaining because their husbands didn't have enough. This is the first time I have heard that a husband has too much. I don't know which one would be worse."

For the first time, Adriana spoke. "My grandmother said that she used to believe in people waiting until marriage to have sex but later realized that it could cause problems if the husband and wife are not sexually compatible. I feel sorry for her because she has found something out way too late."

Melissa, the emerald-green lady, shared her advice. "Green and her husband need to increase their foreplay and use lubrication. A woman's vagina should be comfortable for her husband. She may need to check with her doctor to make sure she doesn't have something else going on."

Chandra spoke again, "Is her real problem about the sex, or is there a part of her that wants to be with her ex-boyfriend?"

"This isn't the first time I have heard women having issues with their husbands being too large for them," Athra shared.

"What advice do you give women in that situation?" Chandra inquired, looking at Athra.

"Melissa gave the best advice," Athra said. "She and her husband both need to relax. I recommend she and her husband incorporate tantric sex in their bedroom."

Athra thought for a moment. "Carlyse, there is a business card in my desk drawer from a couple whose business helps couples with their sex lives. Send their information when you respond to the letter."

"Okay. Next letter," Carlyse announced.

Dear Athra and Group,

My husband likes to role play. I used to enjoy doing it until things began to get a little creepy. Now, he likes for me to dress as a mermaid and only wants to have anal sex. I don't know what to do. He is the only one being satisfied. I am about ready to leave because I don't like the way he makes me feel.

Signed - Red

"Could that be her husband's way of practicing birth control?" a woman in red asked.

Catarina joined the conversation, "It doesn't sound like he is using it as a contraceptive; it sounds like a one-sided situation."

Cilicia interjected, "If her husband only wants anal sex, then something else might be going on with him."

Adriana looked over at her friend. She saw the blank stare in her eyes. Adriana still wondered what exactly happened to Cilicia that made her want to take her own life. She knew Cilicia wasn't telling her everything; she really didn't expect her to. However, it was moments like these that made Adriana cautious of Cilicia's mental health.

"Red needs to talk to her husband and let him know how she feels and what she needs. Reinforcing original boundaries or setting new ones should happen immediately. Finally, I would also recommend couples' and individual therapy at this point. Her husband might be suppressing some things that are impacting their marriage that he may be unconscious of. Something might be surfacing that he feels the only way he can address them is through this type of role play," Athra advised.

Athra paused. "One more thing, Carlyse. Please let her know the Bible does not forbid anal sex between a husband and a wife. Anal sex between women and men was practiced even in ancient times; sculptures and drawings dating back thousands of years are evidence of those practices."

Carlyse summarized the next letter, "This lady writes that her husband is a great father and husband. He provides for her and the children and enjoys family time with them. He sleeps in the guestroom. She talked to her brother about it, and he told her that he heard her husband had been spending time with his buddy from college. She said her brother told her that things probably won't get better because men like that don't change. She signed it, 'Purple'."

"Since she signed her letter purple, I would say she has discovered more than she has put in the letter," Melissa said.

Melissa's comment jarred Adriana. She understood all too well what could be going on in the marriage. She understood that some things Purple could not say or even write about her husband because she wasn't ready to face the possibility of their truths.

"One question she needs answered is what happens when he is with his buddy. She also needs to probe her brother for more details," Chandra suggested.

"Her husband is giving her 85% of what she wants – good provider, great husband, great father. She is missing the sex. The question she must ask herself is how important the sex is to her. I am in no way minimizing the importance of sex in any relationship," Athra said.

"However, would she rather have great sex without being provided for? Great sex without spending time with his family? Great sex with emotional, physical, and/or psychological abuses? Great sex with substance abuses and all the things that come with that? Great sex without any connection at all? All of these are questions we must ask ourselves when we are evaluating whether we should remain in a marriage or relationship that fulfills less than 100% of our needs and desires."

"Answering Chandra's questions will help her determine which

85-15, 70-30, 55-45 she's looking at – where she gets more of what she needs and desires in a marriage or less."

Carlyse finished her notes.

"The last one for the night," Carlyse announced.

Dear Athra and Group,

My wife and I have been married for five years and together for eleven. We decided to have a child six years ago and chose one of our best friends to be the father. I will call him Bruce. My job has always been less demanding, and I always wanted to become a mother, so I was the one to carry the child. We agreed to allow Bruce to be involved in our daughter's life, and he has done a wonderful job. Our daughter was born five months after our wedding. My wife travels with her job, and Bruce helps when she's out of town. The problem we are having is that Bruce and I have grown close to each other, and I am realizing how much I enjoy being with a man and want the traditional family. I am ready to divorce my wife and build a life with Bruce so that our daughter will have a traditional family. I know things would work out with Bruce because we are both bisexual and accept each other just the way we are. The struggle I am having is ending my relationship with my wife. She believes that I should honor the vows I took with her.

Signed - Green"

Another lady in green, who Adriana and Cilicia had not seen before, asked a question. "Was she attracted to Bruce before they had a child?"

The women in the circle all agreed that was a good question. Then some questioned what type of fertilization was used in the pregnancy.

"Had Bruce and Green been sexually involved prior to the agreement for him to become the donor? I imagine Green's wife has a million questions going through her mind right now," came from someone sitting in a red cushioned chair.

Athra adjusted in her seat, "This is a complex situation requiring an equally complex solution. It sounds like Green has already made her decision to leave the marriage. Divorce is a part of life and happens between heterosexual and homosexual couples."

Athra became silent as she pondered the situation.

"Is there anything wrong with Green giving her daughter what she knows is the right thing for her?" Catarina asked. "After all, marriage is supposed to be between a man and a woman. That is what the Bible tells us to do."

Chandra shared her thoughts, "My only concern about this situation is for the child. Green married her wife because she loved her; they made the decision to have a child together, as a lesbian couple. I assume that Green's wife didn't see Bruce as a threat because it was assumed he is a gay man. However, Green has stated that both she and Bruce have accepted their bisexuality. What happens if they begin to live together then realize they were better off in the situations they were in. Then the child is presented with another situation to get used to."

"Are you saying she should stay with her wife?" asked another woman sitting in a red chair.

"No," Chandra began. "I think Green and Bruce need to be clear about who they are before taking a step like this that involves a child. They need to do a lot of soul searching before making this decision."

"They have been searching since their daughter's birth," came the same voice from the same red chair.

Chandra continued her analysis, "It sounds like they are wanting to be together for their daughter. What happens once the child grows up and she doesn't need them as much as she does now? Will that traditional family continue?"

"There is no easy answer here," Athra began. "Any decision they make will leave someone hurt and injured. The first thing I would recommend is individual counseling for Green and Bruce. Then they should have couple's counseling together followed by family counseling. Counseling will help them work through the dynamics of who they are and what it is really like being in a family unit with each other. I am assuming that Green's wife and Bruce have not done the full-time parenting work with Green; therefore, they will face challenges that will need preparation to work through when they come together."

"Are you advising her to leave her wife?" red asked Athra leaning her body forward in her chair.

"It sounds like Green has already made her decision. Going through counseling will help her know if she should follow through with the decision."

Red relaxed in her seat with that answer.

Catarina interjected. "I would advise her to leave her marriage with a woman for the traditional one. That is what Jesus told people to do."

"Traditional in what sense?" Red questioned. "Traditional cover-up marriage, perhaps?"

Catarina became a bit uncomfortable with Red's statement. "That's why I've decided to leave my husband. I feel like I am in a cover-up marriage. I wonder what will happen if we ever have children. Will the sex completely stop."

"That is quite possible," Melissa answered. "You will be surprised at the number of traditionally married people who sleep in separate bedrooms for the sake of the public image."

"I don't want an image," Catarina said.

Carlyse quietly left the room.

"Athra, what did Jesus mean when he told his disciples that some men are eunuchs from their mothers, some from men, and some for religious sake? I believe he was talking about homosexual men and not just men who has been castrated."

Cilicia lifted her head from its resting position; she removed her throw from her shoulders and folded it onto her lap. She was happy Catarina asked the question about that verse. That was one of the verses she had been praying for clarity on.

"You are referring to a chapter in Matthew," Athra began, "somewhere around the 19th chapter. Jesus was having a conversation with his disciples about marriage and divorce. Jesus advised that marriage was created by God for man and woman to become one unit. He said that if a man divorces his wife for any reason other than sexual immorality and marries another woman, he commits adultery. His disciples then questions if they should marry at all if they would commit adultery if they became divorced men.

"Jesus makes it clear that everyone will not be able to accept what he was about to share. Some men are eunuchs because they were born that way, some became eunuchs due to the fact they were made that way by others, and some made the decision because they wanted to work for the kingdom of heaven. He also said for those who can accept it to accept it and for those who can't don't.

"Answering Cilicia's question, I do believe that was the writers' way of addressing not just the physical aspects of being a castrate but also homosexuality. It is well known and documented some people are born with genitalia that does not match a person's sexual identity and/or orientation; this is the first group Jesus was addressing. Some people who were born having outside genitalia that matched their identity and orientation may question their identity and orientation if they have been molested or abused by members of the same or opposite sex; this would be the second group."

Athra paused and took a sip of tea.

"The third group is a bit more complex. Some people who have heightened spiritual awareness experience decreased sexual desire. Devoting oneself to kingdom work on the most elevated level possible here on Earth requires a type of devotion that most people cannot fathom; romantic relationships require the type of attention that a person cannot devote themselves to when they are focusing on their relationship with God; this is also true of parenting. So, people chose celibacy or same sex relationships that can be covered up by their work in the kingdom.

"Jesus was a knowledgeable man; he had learned and observed things during those years that are not mentioned in the Bible that impacted his thoughts about life and influenced his teachings. He had to have known about the scope of work eunuchs performed and what shaped their behaviors."

No one in the group spoke. Athra waited for a couple of minutes.

"Let those who can accept it accept it; let those who cannot accept it rejected it."

Athra waited again. She stood; the group followed her. She extended her arms.

"Our great Creator, we come to you today thanking you for the opportunity to understand ourselves and each other. As we bless your name, and embrace your creation, we ask that you provide healing for every heart that is broken and comfort for those of us in confusion. Remind our sisters and brothers that whatever challenges we are facing, you have already provided the solutions that work for the good of us all. Guide us individually and collectively to your perfect peace as we celebrate this holiday season. So it shall be; and so, it is. AMEN!"

Athra tapped her bowl then circled it three times as she whispered, "For the trinity in us all."

Cilicia approached Catarina at the beverage table. She formally introduced herself.

"I wanted to tell the group that I'm leaving my husband after the holidays," Catarina said. "I don't want to upset everybody right now."

"I'm getting a divorce, too," Cilicia admitted.

They exchanged numbers and made a pact to become each other's support during the process.

Neither Adriana nor Cilicia spoke much on the way home. That meeting was more than they had pictured it would be. As they drove North, the rain stopped, and they could see the waning crescent and stars in the sky. Adriana opened the moonroof of her car to enjoy the spectacle. The sound of the opening brought Cilicia out of her trance. Two objects in the sky shone the brightest and seemed closer than the others.

"Ever since I was a little girl, I would look up in the sky during this time of year to see if God would show us the Star of Bethlehem. I prayed for a revelation that would lead me the way Gabriel led the Magi to Jesus. I have prayed so many prayers asking God to give me a sign and to show me the way. It has finally happened to me. Listening to Athra and the other women have helped me understand. There is a way out of anything if we just know how to find it. God has given us rainbows to remind us there is beauty after the storm passes. We have options that are found within the light; every option is not for everybody. We have to be wise enough and strong within ourselves to live the option that is best for us. The rainbow is more than enough."

22

If You Let Me Stay

Cilicia finally got her day in court. Justus agreed to her returning to the house with the children and her having primary custody; they decided to allow the children to decide when they wanted to spend time with their father.

Cilicia solicited Adriana and Regenia's help in getting resettled before Christmas day. Catarina, who was building her event business, volunteered to help decorate the tree and home. They learned that Catarina's parents had worked on production sets when she was younger but have since retired into the ministry. She shared that her faith had come from spending time with her paternal grandmother in Georgia during summer breaks when she was in elementary and middle schools.

Adriana felt at ease knowing Cilicia was developing a relationship with someone who had similar religious and spiritual beliefs. As they were putting the finishing touches on the railings, Cilicia stepped away to answer her phone.

"Hello," then a pause.

Cilicia placed her right hand on her hips. She paced the catwalk looking over at her children. She eyed the women working on her railings. She focused her attention on Adriana then looked at Catarina. She thought about the 85-15 Support Group and the women there.

"I hear you," she finally said. She stopped her pacing. "I will allow you to come over and have dinner, but you have got to leave within 30 minutes of dinner being over. I don't want to send a wrong message to the children, and I don't want you to get the wrong idea," she emphasized.

"Dinner will be ready in an hour."

Cilicia made her way back down to the bottom of the stairs. She told her friends about the conversation and waited for their comments.

Regenia was the first person to speak; "It is important for children to have a relationship with their father. AND it is also important to have clear, defined boundaries when going through a divorce. Be careful of the messages you send him."

"I told him he needed to leave within thirty minutes of dinner being over. I don't want him getting the wrong idea."

Catarina added, "Make sure you don't spend too much time with him. My counselor told me that men can get the wrong idea even when we have told them what we mean."

"Thanks for the advice," Cilicia said. "I have never had to go through anything like this, and I don't want him to get the wrong message."

"He is getting used to a new way of living, too," Catarina said. "It will be a little tricky, but I'm here for support."

Adriana pledged her support, too. She was feeling a bit uneasy about Justus being around. She looked at her phone and thought about calling Gavin to join them. She thought about what her mother said about getting the wrong message; Gavin being with them might send the message that this holiday season was like all the others. She put her phone back in her pocket.

Alexus and Ariadne helped Regenia put the finishing touches on dinner. Cilicia joined them and informed Alexus that her father would be joining them for dinner.

"Why would you let him come here without asking Evian and me how we feel?" Alexus questioned, looking at her mother with fear in her eyes.

"He said that he wants to spend time with you and your brother."

"I won't be here," Alexus said. "I'll eat in my room." She stormed out of the kitchen.

Minutes later the doorbell rang. Cilicia sent Evian to answer the door. She was still contemplating what Alexus said. She knew her daughter had been avoiding her father since the last day they were in this house. She didn't push the issue while they were at Adriana's house, and she wasn't sure she should push the issue now.

Justus came in admiring the beautiful Christmas decorations as he followed Evian into the family room. The Hornets were playing the Warriors, who always excited Justus. He sat in his favorite chair and put his feet on the ottoman that was in front of it.

Regenia adjusted the tie on her apron as she walked into the family room to speak to Justus and to announce dinner was ready. She whispered to Cilicia as she returned to the kitchen, "You can't let people get too comfortable," then motioned to Justus just before he rose from his position.

Justus and the boys had positioned themselves at the table to continue to watch the game during dinner. Justus wasn't surprised Alexus wasn't at the table; she had been ghosting whenever he was present. However, Catarina caught him off guard.

Straightening his posture into a defensive position he asked, "Who's this?"

"I'm Cilicia's friend Catarina."

"How did y'all meet?" Justus asked.

"We met in a book club," Catarina answered as she moved closer to the table.

"Book club group?" Justus asked. "When did you join a book club?" he questioned looking at Cilicia.

"I joined a while ago," Cilicia answered.

Regenia held her arms out. "Let's bless the food." She bowed her head.

Nicklous said grace, "Thank you for this food we are about to receive. Let it provide nourishment to our bodies and uplift our souls in Jesus's name. Amen."

It was clear throughout dinner that Justus was uncomfortable with Cilicia's new friend.

He asked questions about the title of the book – *A Daily Sip of Joy and Peace* by Elanor Hooks.

Where did the book club meet – The Enlightened Living Ministries – The ELM.

What motivated Cilicia to join – to maintain peace in her storm.

He wanted to know why Catarina was there. It was clear from the tone of his voice and the changes in his demeanor that he didn't like the changes that had occurred.

"You never hired a decorator before," he said to Cilicia.

"It was a gift," Cilicia. "She wanted to help us get settled in before Christmas."

Justus pinched his lips together and drummed the fingers on his left hand beside his plate. He looked around the table. "Is Alexus eating tonight?"

"She said she wasn't hungry," Cilicia answered.

Adriana and Regenia cleared everyone's dinner plate and replaced it with dessert – apple pie ala mode.

Very little was said during dessert. Everyone was on their phone or, in Regenia's case, watching the game. The half-time buzzer caused Justus to look at the television. He finished his dessert then stood up from his seat; he carried his dish into the kitchen.

"Evian, I'm leaving. I need to get back to watch the second half of the game," Justus announced. He and Evian walked to the door.

Two minutes later, Cilicia's phone pinged.

"I don't appreciate you letting strangers in my house."

She didn't respond to the message.

"You need to talk to me before you go making decisions like that."

Cilicia put the phone back in her pocket, but it didn't stop the pings from coming in. She walked over to Adriana.

"Would it be okay if we joined you for Christmas? I don't want to deal with him and our families right now," she said with tears and fear in her eyes.

"No problem. Are you going to be okay here tonight?"

"I'll be okay," Cilicia said.

Catarina walked over but didn't say anything. Cilicia didn't need her to. She knew she had a new friend. Catarina was confident and refused to allow Justus to intimidate her. That was one thing he didn't like in women – their refusal to cow down to him.

The ladies watched a Christmas Classic – *This Christmas*. Evian and Nicklous finished watching the game in Evian's room. Alexus didn't want any company, so Ariadne ended up watching the movie, too.

* * *

Cilicia was happy to be in her own home. She stretched her body across the sofa. Then she turned on the television and opened her favorite streaming application. She searched for shows until she heard Stevie Nicks, a singer her father's rebellious younger sister used to listen to when she was young.

Cilicia recalled the joys of having her aunt home from California. She always told the wildest stories and seemed so carefree. Everyone knew she was the black sheep of the family. However, Cilicia always admired her courage for living life on her own terms. So, she clicked on the show and began to watch it.

The introduction of the show gave her something to think about. The lead character said that people are never who they say they are or who they seem to be; that everyone's life is out of control in its own way. She wondered if her life was out of control when she married Justus twenty years ago. Could her separation be the product of what was always her reality?

A familiar loneliness came over her. She wasn't exactly sure where it began, but she knew how she needed it to end. She picked up her phone and read the messages that came through before everyone left.

One of the problems I always had with you was that you don't know how to give me the respect you need to. You needed to talk to me before you let a stranger decorate my house.

It was clear from the tone of the message he was still angry.

You might think that you will be better off without me, but you will see how much you need me. You can't do NOTHING without me.

Cilicia shook her head. "Please."

Things would be different between us if you just understood how you need to love a man. I don't know what kind of relationship your parents had. Maybe you didn't get the right message on what you needed to do to keep a man.

Cilicia laughed at that one.

If you want to talk to me about how we can work things out, I might be willing to be back for Christmas. But you will need to make some changes and come to me with a plan like a wife should.

Cilicia was shocked by that message. During this entire messaging, he still acted as if he had negotiating power. Apparently, he had forgotten they had been to court and received a legal separation. There was nothing to negotiate.

* * *

Cilicia was apprehensive about meeting Adriana and Sheraton for their annual holiday shopping trip to South Park Mall. They did little talking as they rushed through the crowd in search of the best deals. Both Adriana and Sheraton chose not to purchase a gift for their husbands; this was the tradition they chose to break. Instead, they focused on finding the perfect gift for their mothers and daughters. By 4:30, they were headed uptown to 7th Restaurant & Lounge for an early dinner.

The trio began to feel the awkwardness of the season once they were able to settle into their seats. An order for their usual drinks, two Cosmopolitans and a classic Margarita, was placed as soon as the waiter arrived.

They talked about the gifts they had already purchased and how happy they were for shopping to be over. Three sips of their drinks, then the moment everyone had feared arrived.

Cilicia looked at Sheraton, "When were you going to tell us that you and Winston have been swinging with our husbands?"

"First off, I never said I was swinging with your husbands. Second thing is that some things need to stay between married couples," Sheraton answered.

"We're your friends," Cilicia shot back at her.

"What's between you and Justus and Adriana and Gavin is none of our business, so our business is none of yours."

Adriana was astonished, yet thrilled, to see this side of Sheraton.

"When you decided to swing with our husbands, you made it our business," Cilicia argued.

"When I decided to go to swinging parties with MY husband, it was our business. Who chose to go with their husbands and wives was not OUR business."

"We are your friends, Sheraton," Cilicia beseeched her.

"Here is the hard truth – people do things with and without their spouses' knowledge. Some people's spouse may be fully aware of what is going on and choose not to participate. Some people's spouse may not know what they are doing. We all know that what happens at those parties stays at those parties."

Sheraton lifted her glass and took another sip of her drink. "Now, I'm done talking about it."

The conversation between Cilicia and Sheraton was not what Adriana needed when she was trying her best to find her way back to Gavin. Throughout the entire dialogue, she was trying to find that place of peace and security this time of year always brought that added strength to their marriage. She had been searching for any glimmer of hope in the darkness she had been feeling. She absentmindedly dunked into the creamy collard greens dip.

"What about you and Shanica?"

"Not that it's any of your business; I will tell you about us. Shanica was my college roommate. We rekindled our relationship after the twins were born," Sheraton answered Cilicia.

"Wow," Adriana commented, "that's a long time."

"My marriage was feeling crowded once the twins were born. Winston and Justus were spending more time at the office; even when Winston was home, they were always on the phone about something. It seemed like Winston wasn't helping as much as he did when the kids were first born. I started feeling like I didn't have any space in my own life. So, when Shanica's job moved her to Charlotte, we started hanging out again," Sheraton explained.

"Does Winston know how deep your relationship with Shanica is?" Adriana inquired.

"Yes; he's always known."

"How does he feel about it?" Adriana asked.

"We understand each other."

"What does that mean?" Cilicia asked.

"Winston and I understand each other and accept it."

Cilicia's eyes got big. "Ohh, My, God. You knew the whole time about Justus and Winston," she said slapping her hand on the table. "You knew!"

Adriana closed her eyes as her heart sank. She was getting herself ready to hear what she had dreaded the most.

"Did you know about Gavin, too?" Cilicia said pointing at Adriana.

"Know what?" Sheraton asked.

"Know that he is gay, too."

"Wait a minute," Sheraton said. "I never said that."

"Yes; you did," Cilicia said.

"I said that Winston and I understand and accept who we are. It has nothing to do with you or Adriana. I'm talking about my marriage," Sheraton said.

"I can't believe you right now," Cilicia said leaning into the table. "I thought you were our friend."

"I am your friend," Sheraton.

"Friends don't do the things you have done. Friends don't keep secrets like this. Friends protect each other," Cilicia said.

"Friends respect people's personal space," Sheraton added.

Two orders of chicken and red velvet waffles and an order of shrimp & grits arrived. The trio began to eat albeit slowly. No one made eye contact. No one spoke. What was there left to say?

When the waiter checked in on the table, Adriana requested boxes. Their appetites had left them.

Adriana broke the silence as they were driving home. "You and Shanica seemed very comfortable in the 85-15 Group. How long have you been going?"

"We've been going for a year or so."

"Are the women who attend lesbians?" Adriana asked.

Sheraton laughed. "No; some are but most I would say are not."

"Did Shanica turn you out like a lot of roommates do?" Cilicia asked.

"No," Sheraton began, "it happened to me like it happens to a lot of people."

"What's that?" Cilicia asked.

"A family member did it when I was about seven years old." Sheraton eyes drew a blank stare.

"My parents used to have poker parties to make ends meet. My aunt used to help at the parties and help herself to me," Sheraton concluded.

Neither Cilicia nor Adriana responded to that comment.

"It might not be seven, but it's usually a family member who crosses those boundaries," Adriana thought to herself.

"Justus is in a detox program," Sheraton said.

"What?" Cilicia and Adriana said at the same time.

"I thought you might want to know that he is trying to get himself together. Winston told me about it a couple of days ago."

* * *

Adriana was happy Gavin would be home when she got there. The last time she felt this amount of intensity in her root chakra was the first time Gavin kissed her. She noticed that the flame began burning as Cilicia talked about Sheraton and Shanica's relationship. Although she tried her best to block out the things Cilicia was saying, "Have you ever dreamed what it would be like to grind on another woman? Would that be better than the scissor position? I bet that would be the one to have the best orgasm." brought back thoughts of the days she and Gavin used to watch Kama Sutra videos and practiced the positions.

Cilicia was quiet for a few minutes. Then she began again. "I've always wondered what exactly a woman could do for another woman that a man could not."

She smiled a devilish smile, "I used to have lesbian dreams before I met Justus; he killed all those fantasies. We used to have fun. He used to fulfill all my desires. He made me forget about everything and everyone else." By the time she finished her thoughts, the devilish smile turned into sadness.

Although the thought of Sheraton and Shanica being in bed together sparked the flame, Adriana knew she wanted and needed Gavin to put it out. The flame began to move up to her sacral chakra and was growing in intensity. Just imagining the things Cilicia was saying was what she needed to put a spark back into her bedroom.

"Shanica is a very attractive woman; I can see how any man or woman would be drawn into her high cheekbones, light brown eyes, and full lips. When she swooped her braids over the breasts, I looked at them. She is very alluring," Cilicia admitted.

Adriana looked over at Cilicia with an inquiring smile. She was happy to hear Cilicia direct her focus on Sheraton and Shanica instead of their husbands. But still, she could not ignore the flame that was burning inside of her and Cilicia's curiosity.

"I agree that Shanica is a beautiful woman. Her beauty could be intimidating and alluring. Does that mean you are attracted to her?"

"It simply means I can see how Sheraton would be drawn into her when they were in college; that's all."

Adriana, trying to not focus on her condition, spoke again, "Sheraton was right when she said that people are dynamic, and marriages are not what we see on television or even what we witnessed as children. All we see is the way society tells us how people and marriages should be, but everything is much more complex than that. The behind-the-scenes situations is where the depth is and are the glue that keeps things together."

Cilicia commented, "Or make things fall apart."

* * *

Cilicia woke up to a ping from her phone.

I would like to come over and be with the kids this morning.

Cilicia sat up in her bed. "I'm really not ready to deal with this so early in the morning," she said aloud. She rubbed her eyes.

The children need to know that we are still a family even though I am not living in the house right now.

The message angered Cilicia a bit; it had been years since Justus wanted to act like they were a family. He only found it convenient when it was for a public image he needed. She decided to send a "Merry Christmas" text to her family and friends.

I know I haven't been the husband you needed me to be over the past few years. I let things get in the way of our marriage. I just want you to know that I have completed a detox program, and I go to a rehab program after work. I want the chance to prove to you that I can be the man you need me to be. I am sorry about everything. If you let me come over this morning, I can start showing you how much I've changed.

Cilicia wanted to believe him; she wanted to be back in his arms again. But she thought about how he made her feel the last time they were in this house. She thought about the last two times he left and came back – the first time he had found God again, and the second time he promised to go to church and work on their sex life. She didn't know then what she had seen over the past fourteen months. She began to cry.

"What will I be saying to Alexus if I let him come back? What will I be saying to myself if I let him come back? What if he has really changed?"

Cilicia walked into her bathroom. She looked in the mirror at the streaks on her face.

"Pull yourself together, girl. Your love is too genuine and pure to be thrown back in your face," she said to herself.

We are going to Adriana and Gavin's around 1:00. You can see the children there.

Cilicia thought about the advice Regenia gave her. She wanted her family to be together; however, she was tired of the loneliness and humiliation. Even today, on this Christmas day, she was struggling to put the tears back where they belonged before seeing her children. She knew she needed to straighten her face and put back on the mask she had been wearing for years.

* * *

Christmas at the Matthews house was merry and bright. Regenia enjoyed putting the finishing touches on the Carrot Cake Cheesecake and Red Velvet cake with Alexus and Ariadne. Adriana and Cilicia worked on the side dishes.

Cilicia told Adriana and Regenia about the text messages Justus sent and her response.

"I don't want to send him the wrong message," Cilicia said.

Adriana looked at her mother. "You did the right thing," Regenia said.

The tables were completely set. Adriana and Cilicia enjoyed eggnog while the children taste-tested Regenia's punch. Gavin and his dad tried to sneak in as much football as possible before sitting in the dining room.

When the prime rib was ready, Adriana called Gavin into the kitchen to finish the entree'.

"I thought you said Justus was coming," Gavin whispered to her as she handed him the knife and fork for cutting.

"That's what I was told. We've tried to stall, but we can't wait forever. Everyone is ready to eat," Adriana said.

Dinner and dessert were over, and still Justus had not come. Adriana decided to go ahead with the gift exchange.

"I'm glad he didn't come," Cilicia said to Adriana and Regenia. "Alexus had said she was not going to eat with us if he came."

"Is she still angry with him?" Regenia asked.

"Yes; she's said that if he comes back home, she will graduate early. She doesn't want to be around him," Cilicia said.

"Just give her some time," Regenia advised. "She's in a tough time in her life – wanting to be independent yet knowing she is not quite ready. Don't forget that you are her mother and one day she will be gone. Whatever decisions you make from here on out, you must think about what you want for yourself."

Cilicia felt puzzled. Was Regenia trying to advise her to stay with Justus?

"I'm not saying that you need to stay with your husband if that is not the right thing for you. You will have to make decisions about your future whether you follow through with your divorce or change your mind. Honor her as much as you can but make decisions that will also be right for you in the long run."

Cilicia felt relief at Regenia's explanation. "I wish I could talk to my mother the way I talk to you."

"Give that some time, too," Regenia said.

A spa day, a bottle of wine, and gold beaded bracelet with a heart-shaped charm that read, "God is my strength, and I have hope." were gifts Adriana and Regenia gave Cilicia.

"I know it might not seem like it now, but you will come out of this on the other side of the rainbow once the storm clears," Regenia said to Cilicia with a hug and kiss on her cheek.

Tear welled up in Cilicia's eyes. "It's so hard."

"Strength is never easy," Regenia said. "Through it all, God is always with us."

* * *

Gavin was still feeling the distance between him and Adriana despite this being one of her favorite times of the year. He had given her a gift she had been wanting since their tenth anniversary – diamond studded earrings from Tiffany's. She was excited about the gift; however, he could tell that something was still missing inside of her.

When Adriana got out of the shower and walked towards her bedroom, she heard Mariah Carey's "All I Want for Christmas Is You" playing. She was surprised to hear her favorite Christmas song playing. She smiled, and her eyes began to glow.

Then she looked at her vanity chair. Lying on the back was a Mrs. Santa Claus nightie with a hat and white furry shoes. She dropped her towel and put on the outfit.

When she got into her bedroom, Gavin was lying on the bed in his Mr. Santa outfit. He held his hand out for her.

"All I want for Christmas is my wife," he said.

* * *

It had been two days since Cilicia heard from Justus when he came to the house. She was reluctant to open the door because she did not know what to expect from him.

She questioned him about not showing up at Adriana's house on Christmas. He told her that he decided to go to his parents' house instead. Cilicia doubted what he said because she knew he wouldn't want to face his parents this soon in their divorce process, especially since he was still trying to get her to take him back.

She told him that the children were still in bed; she was allowing them to sleep in during the break.

"You're making Evian lazy by letting him sleep in this late," he said to her.

"It's only eleven; kids have a lot more to think about and worry about than we did when we were kids," she said in her son's defense.

"We had problems, too. It's no different."

"We weren't expected to learn as much or do as much as these students do today. So, letting him sleep will be okay."

Justus remained silent for a few moments.

"Look, Cilicia. Evian needs his dad and so does Alexus. We need to work things out for our kids. God gave children two parents so they both can raise them. We had both of our parents when we were growing up and still do," Justus pleaded with his wife.

"Have you forgotten about the past few years? Did you forget about what you did to me? What you drove me to?" Cilicia questioned him.

"We don't need to bring up the past. We just need to think about right now and the future."

"The past is what brought us to the right now and will determine our future. It's over between us."

"We made a promise to God. Vows are not to be broken, Cilicia."

"You broke the vows, Justus. You abandoned your marriage while we were still living under the same roof."

"Do you think anybody else will want you? No man is going to want to put up with you. I'm the only one who will put up with your craziness and bipolar behavior."

Justus's remarks hit Cilicia in her gut. "Get the fuck out, you bastard. LEAVE NOW!!!"

She walked towards the door; Justus did not follow her. "You're not welcomed here anymore."

"I'm not leaving until we settle this."

"It is already settled. I'm done trying with you," Cilicia firmly stated.

Justus got off his seat and advanced towards her. Determined that this would be her last physical fight with him, Cilicia braced herself to give Justus something he would never forget. He reached for her neck; Cilicia jumped and kicked him in his stomach before his grip could take hold. He was about to hit her again when he looked up and saw Alexus grabbing a knife.

"Get off, Mama, or I'll kill you!" Alexus promised her father.

"Daddy," Evian said. "What are you doing?"

Justus lowered his arms then walked to the door and left.

Cilicia, who was sitting on the floor, put her face in her hands and began to cry. She felt ashamed that her children needed to defend her against their father. And, because her children needed to protect her, she knew what she had to do to protect them. She got off the floor and hugged her children, then she went to her room.

* * *

Adriana and Regenia were there in less than thirty minutes. Adriana knocked on Cilicia's bedroom door then let herself in.

"Alexus called Mama," Adriana said as she approached Cilicia's bed. "Are you okay?"

Cilicia turned and looked at her. "I'm okay."

"Do you need to come to the house?"

"No; I'm staying in my own house. I'm through with him, Adriana," Cilicia began to cry again. "My children had to defend me against him. No child should have to get involved in their parents' fight. He will never change, and I am never taking him back."

Adriana sat on the bed beside her friend and hugged her. "We'll always be here for you."

Making the Rainbow Enough

Choice; we all have a choice;
From one light; the prism separates
To display the beauty of all there is;
God created the rainbow to celebrate diversity;
One person's choice is not always right for another;
But we are still ONE from the same divine light.

The rainbow has to be enough;
It is not going anywhere;
That is what makes it so beautiful;
It comes to us to remind us that
We have a choice.

We can choose what is right for us;
While someone else makes a diverse choice;
It does not mean we are less than or they are more than;
It simply means that we can choose and still be ONE!

23

Compassion

Athra was waiting for Cilicia when Carlyse announced her arrival. Athra had learned about the situation after Christmas from Adriana when they had lunch earlier in the week. Athra had been praying for Cilicia since she learned about the difficulties she had been facing. Athra knew that divorcing a person who seemed to have narcissism symptoms would be a challenge.

Cilicia came in and relaxed herself on the lounge chair. She took three deep breaths and exhaled. "I am just realizing that I have been in fight and flight mode for the past decade." She began to cry. "I don't want to do this anymore. I can't do this anymore."

Athra sat silently as Cilicia released all that she had pinned up inside of her.

"It doesn't matter to me if he has a sponsor or following an AA program; I cannot go back to where I allowed him to take me. I have never been a fighter; I had promised myself that I would never let a man do to me what I saw my dad do to my mother." She wiped her nose.

Cilicia stood up and began to pace the floor. "I almost let him break me down, beat me down. No; I wasn't like my mother because she didn't fight back. I know my daughter saw him rape me; I can see it in her eyes. I saw it when she pulled a knife on him." She wiped the tears from her face.

Athra stood up and began to approach her.

Cilicia held her hand out. "I'm okay; I'm finding in me the strength God gave me when I was a little girl and saw my dad kick my mom." She stopped pacing.

"I won't let Alexus think she is supposed to allow a man to treat her this way. I won't let Evian think he is supposed to treat his wife, the mother of his children, this way."

She smiled to herself.

"We're going to be okay. I just got to get us to the other side of this," Cilicia said. She took a deep breath then sat down.

She leaned her head against the back of the chair. She put her hands together in a praying position. Athra continued her silence. When Cilicia lowered her hands, she began to speak.

"Would you like to share what happened?" Athra asked.

Cilicia gave her an account of what happened the last time Justus was at the house. Then she added, "Even after all of that, he is still sending condescending text messages and asking for us to get back together. He said that he has been going to church and working with someone on his anger management."

"How does that make you feel?"

"I feel like he is lying to get back into my life. I know I can't trust what he says because he has never changed after all of these years of forgiveness."

"Does that mean you are going forward with your divorce?"

"Yes; I feel like that is the only choice I have right now." She sat in deep thought.

Athra gave Cilicia space to process all that was going on in her mind and spirit. She remembered what it felt like going through her own divorce; she remembered the courage it took for her to walk away from a dream that she had to accept had gone from her.

"The 85-15 Group feels more like 85% of what I don't want and 15% of what I do want," Cilicia finally said.

"Yes; Athra said. "Some women are there because their marriage is more of what they don't want."

"I thought the group was all about women who are married to men who are having sex with men."

"That was how the group got started over a decade ago; however, it has evolved to include women who are facing challenges in their marriage regardless of the reason."

"I have been thinking about what you said about Jesus's response about eunuchs, and it made me think about a colleague who alluded to the fact that he was homosexual because of his relationship with a youth minister who also happened to be a family member." Cilicia sat in silence.

"I have been wondering if something happened to Justus in his childhood."

Athra took a deep breath. Cilicia took that as a sign that she needed to relax to hear what Athra had to say.

"I came across a sermon on day, and the minister said that when women talk about trusting a man, she is talking about fidelity; however, when a man talks about trust he is speaking of something different. He said that men are meaning they cannot trust that their wives or significant other would still love them if they revealed certain truths about their childhoods. Society teaches men to mask the things that traumatized them in childhood because it makes them seem weak. Some men release their frustrations in unhealthy ways – promiscuity, alcohol and drug abuse, violence, and even suicide. Even gambling habits, overspending, and child abuse are attempts at managing pain."

Athra paused to give Cilicia a chance to comment. Cilicia remained silent.

Athra continued, "Men, just like women, are struggling to reconcile their past with the lives they are living in the present. Women are allowed to feel things that society tells men emasculates them if they feel them; therefore, women find comfort in other women by talking. Women even find comfort and security in the arms of their husbands or significant others and support groups like the 85-15. Sometimes, women choose to empower themselves by becoming promiscuous because they finally have control over their own lives and can make choices. Other times people find healing in religion, spirituality, energy work, volunteer work, and even non-profits.

"Men, on the other hand, find comfort in other men. Sometimes it involves sex, but most of the time it does not."

Athra paused then smiled.

"What are you thinking about?" Cilicia asked.

"Whenever I used to say negative things about men, my father used to stay, 'Women, too.' It was his way of letting me know that we all suffer the same things and attempt to heal ourselves in the same way," she shared, then smiled again.

"I've come to accept and understand that he was wise in that statement. We all are in the same boat trying to heal and overcome the same things."

"I never thought that Justus's frustrations might be linked to his childhood being more like mine. I never even imagined it could be true."

"Men are sometimes marrying women for protection just like women marry men for protection. In one way or another, we are all working to heal from our past. If people are working with positive energy, then our marriages and long-term relationships do help us heal; however, if we are working with negative energy, then we cause more pain for ourselves and the ones we love. Just imagine what the world would be like if men could share their deepest secrets with the woman they love; our world would be a much better place."

"I am still confused about the fact that Moses allowed people to get a divorce whereas Jesus said it goes against God's plan. I am trying my best to understand all of this," Cilicia said.

"Based on what we read in the Bible, both Moses and Jesus said that divorce goes against God's original plan at creation; God created man and woman to join as one to procreate. We must keep in mind that it was at the beginning of creation when the world needed to be populated. Earth now has over eight billion people, and we are putting a strain on our natural resources. Therefore, we need to adjust our mindsets for the present day instead of trying to live by laws that were created when Homo sapiens were in their infancy.

"I am sure that God's plan included forgiveness for divorce, such as sexual immorality as it is written in the Bible from both Moses and Jesus. The issue of abuse was not addressed because it was common for men to treat their wives in ways that we consider to be abusive today. That is a testament to our spiritual, emotional, and psychological evolution.

"Moses also said that people's hearts become hardened, which was another reason for divorce in the Old Testament. When our hearts become hardened, the way we interact and engage changes, too.

"I think about the law of inertia when I help people work through some of their most challenging situations. It's how I reasoned myself to peace."

Athra sat silently as Cilicia processed what she said.

"Remind me about the law of inertia; I know it's something I studied in school."

"Basically, anything that is at rest, such as our peace, will stay that way until a force causes it to move. In your case, it is the things going on in your marriage that are causing you to move. The other part of the law says that whatever is in motion will continue to move in that direction until an equal and opposite force causes it to change direction. Again, the situation in your marriage," Athra said.

"Wow, I never thought about relationships that way," Cilicia acknowledged.

"Everything in the universe operates that way. Adriana and Sheraton have chosen to remain married because there is not a force great enough to make them want to get a divorce. On the other hand, you and Catarina have encountered a force that is much greater than the love you have for your husbands," Athra described.

"Could it be that Justus's heart became harden towards me which is why he became abusive in our marriage?"

"I doubt he became abusive because his heart was hardened towards you since the abuse began so early in your marriage. In my experience, I have learned that people who display abuse so early in relationships are already having issues within themselves. That abuse is inflicted on the person in front of them because they cannot, for one reason or another, take it out on who or what created their pain."

Athra rose from her chair, walked to her bookshelf, then handed Cilicia the book.

"My brother gave me this book when I was going through my divorce. He told me that it would help me understand the dynamics of my relationship with my husband. He told me to focus on healing myself in the process of learning to let go of what I could not change in my ex-husband."

"Does that mean that Moses understood things about marriage that Jesus didn't?"

"Based on what we read in the Bible, I would say Moses had knowledge about things that Jesus did not know. Moses was forty years old when he left Egypt; he had forty years of being formally educated and gaining knowledge from the work he did for pharaoh.

He would have a more in-depth view of life than Jesus did when we look at things in the physical and logical sense. Moses was older than Jesus when he left Egypt; therefore, that could've made him a bit wiser. Thirty-three at the time of death is still very young. I imagine Moses knew how destructive staying in a marriage that had run its course could be to individuals and how that destruction could and would extend into society."

Athra smiled again.

"Let me in on the secret," Cilicia said, smiling back.

"I was just thinking of Medusa."

"Medusa?"

"Yes; Medusa."

Athra paused.

"We've all heard about her. Mythology tells us that her hair was made of snakes and that anyone who looked upon her face and made eye contact would die. What is not as mainstream is the story of how she got that way.

"One of the stories is that Medusa, who was a mortal, was in Athena's temple worshipping the goddess. Poseidon, Athena's husband, saw Medusa and thought she was very beautiful, so he seduced and impregnated her. When Athena found out what Poseidon had done, she became enraged with Medusa. Due to her anger, Athena cursed Medusa for Poseidon's transgressions. She turned her hair into snakes and killed any man who looked upon her beauty. That's it; that's one of the stories," Athra smiled.

"Wow," Cilicia said with her eyes opened wide. "I never knew that."

"What if Moses knew of stories that were like that and were indeed true? We are told he had access to the world's largest library at the time. He lived closer to the time the Greek, Roman, and Nordic gods were alive. What if there is some truth to the god's behaviors and their wives' jealousy and revenge on mortal women and men. Wouldn't it make sense for them to get a divorce. Wouldn't a peaceful person rather see another solution to the problem than putting a nasty curse on someone who was helpless and powerless?" Athra asked.

"Am I wrong for questioning God?"

"People often confuse questioning things written in the Bible with questioning God. We must remember that God has been revealing knowledge to both men and women throughout time, and these truths have been written in many books all over the world.

"Some people even feel that asking questions is dangerous; however, Jesus, his disciplines, and priests, such as Nicodemus, debated things all the time. That's why we see the commentary in Matthew surrounding the issue of marriage. It is okay to ask questions to gain a better understanding of anything."

"Do I have to worry about damnation when I follow through with my divorce?"

"Moses had written a law in the Old Testament that allowed people to get a divorce because of human nature; marriages have always been a challenge for people. The very things that make marriages challenging today made marriages challenging tens of thousands of years ago – infidelity, finances, abuses, loss of attraction, incompatibility. In the New Testament Jesus advises men to not marry if they understand they were not ready to make the commitment because they are still human. God is fully aware of the fact humans cannot live by every law that has ever been written in any holy text. God knows we are doing the best we can until we have gained more knowledge and become wiser. That is why Jesus taught the "The Lord's Prayer". Forgiveness by God for everyone."

Cilicia gave a long sigh.

"Most people marry when they are very young, acting out of emotion. Love is important, but it does not keep people together."

"How should a person look at what Moses and Jesus said about marriage and divorce?" Cilicia questioned.

"Moses, being the statesman he was in Egypt, would've had knowledge of what happened in other civilizations that helped people live more peaceful, including allowing people to get a divorce. He would've known that people chose murder or deceit, especially towards women, when it was time to end a marriage. Maybe he thought that his law was a better way to live. Likewise, Jesus might have encounter other societies and civilizations whose existence were more peaceful by people remaining married or not marrying at all.

"There are so many questions that we are too far removed from to truly answer. Maybe we should focus a little more on living in our present time instead of trying to make our lives fit into a history and culture that have long passed us."

Athra paused, "I'm not saying that we should not study history to learn from other people's experiences; I am saying that we should look at who we are and what is going on in present day, just as Moses and Jesus did, and make decisions that are best for our people in the time we are living in. People are more educated than they were back then; roles have changed, which mean people have changed. If we want to make our lives and society better, then sometimes divorce is necessary."

"You have given me a lot to think about," Cilicia said. She held the book out. "I'm going to read this book, too."

"Remember you are on a journey, so be patient with yourself. Be patient with your children because they are going through their own journey."

Athra rose from her seat as Cilicia collected her things.

On her drive home, Cilicia began to experience feelings of guilt; she felt as if she had failed at something in her marriage. Then, she thought about her children. She knew she could not change anyone's past, including her own. However, she could influence the future by the way she parented and interacted with her children.

24

Letting Go of Pain

Adriana entered the walking trail. She stopped then used her phone to search for Terence Trent D'Arby who had become Sananda Maitreya; she found the video from his 1995 concert in London that would sum up how she was feeling. She did more stretches as she let the advertisements play.

As soon as the lead guitarist hit the first note, she was ready to begin her walk. She needed the soulful, raspy yet sultry sound of TTD's voice to help her release those things she needed to shed if she was going to allow Gavin to continue to provide the healing in her life. She knew God had sent him to do just that.

One of the last things her father said to her before his death was to let go of her past once and for all.

"Men know when their wives are holding on to someone else," Marvin said to his daughter. "That makes him feel like he's not enough, and all men need to know he is enough for his wife, that he can provide everything she needs. Let that Jamie go once and for all."

CONFUSION, COMPASSION, CONFESSION - 223

She thought about the first time she heard the song. It was the summer between her junior and senior years. Courtney told her she had been listening to that song because she was trying to let go of a situation she didn't need to be in. Courtney didn't share the details because Adriana needed to get herself together to go back to school. Adriana remembered how broken and unloved the situation with Jamie had left her feeling.

Tears began to flow from Adriana's eyes. She had been holding on to more of the pain from her relationship with Jamie than she realized. She increased the pace of her walk as Sananda's pain allowed her to feel the hurt she had still been holding on to. The past year revealed more feelings about Jamie than she realized still existed. She could not think about Gavin without something about her relationship with Jamie creeping into her mind.

She stopped in her tracks as the song reached its bridge. She bent over and rested her hands on her knees. She walked over to a tree to support herself. She let it all out. She didn't fight back the tears that she had held in for over twenty years.

Jamie had been the unrequited love that secretly kept a place in her heart. Although she had physically moved on from Jamie, a part of her was still with him. She could finally allow herself to feel the heartbreak and disappointment that her family and college life would not allow her to acknowledge back then.

She opened herself to feel the love she still had for him and to image what life would've been like with their child that would forever be lost in the abyss. She allowed herself to wish, for just a moment, that things could've been different between them.

Adriana didn't block herself from remembering how he felt inside of her for he had been the first time she experienced sex with so much passion and love. He brought the woman out of her every time he touched her.

She asked herself if confronting Gavin with what she found and

Cilicia's accusations and her losing Gavin meant she would lose Jamie again. The time between Jamie and Gavin was a period where she streamed one-night stands and two-off encounters in search of the feelings she got from Jamie. It wasn't until she allowed herself to surrender to Gavin's love that she again enjoyed sex the way she had with Jamie.

Adriana looked at her phone and played the video again. She listened to the gentleness in his speaking voice and looked into his eyes. She thought about how gentle Gavin had always been with her; how he had always tried to make her life as easy as possible.

She remembered the day she threw the remote control at him before Ariadne was born when a part of her was still longing for Jamie. She could not tell him what was wrong with her, so she said that she didn't want to be married anymore. She told him that she wished she was closer to home. That was when he made the decision to transition to the reserve instead of active duty.

That day she realized that she was still living in the fantasy of Jamie, so she suppressed any thoughts or feelings of him until Cilicia started bringing things up about their husbands. Adriana shook her head.

Gavin's love for her was real; it was giving her all that she had hoped and prayed for even before she knew there was a Gavin Douglass Matthews. As she listened to Sananda sing about needing to let go of what wasn't real in his life, she allowed the power of his voice to take a hold of her mind and heart as if Gavin was drawing her back into him.

Adriana recalled what Athra told her the last time they had a session, "You must spend some time in your pain if you are going to understand and heal from it. Ignoring the pain and pretending that it never existed opens one to the possibility of repeating it or transferring it to our children or grandchildren. Covering it up leads to lies, mental health issues, and substance abuse."

She pushed herself from the tree to continue her walk. She was happy the trail was still empty because she needed the space to let go of the pain. She listened to different performances of "Holding on to You".

* * *

Adriana finally reached Ilios Noches. She did not know the restaurant had moved to Providence Road. As she crossed the parking lot to the entrance, she could not miss the physique standing in the outdoor seating area.

The five feet, eleven inches stood with his hands behind his back. The slim-fitted, royal blue, button-down shirt could not hide the toned torso it covered. Her eyes followed the shirt's tail to the black slim-fitted jeans. Something in Adriana pulsated as her eyes looked upon his face. Their eyes locked. Adriana's lip expanded into a smile and so did Jamie's.

"I see you still shop at Banana Republic," Adriana said when she reached him.

"Occasionally," he replied admiring the beauty that was in front of him.

He reached to hug her but paused. "I'm sorry."

Tears welled up in Adriana's eyes; she batted them back to where they belonged. "I know." She leaned in for the hug she had been craving for over two decades.

It was not a hug; it was an embrace. Adriana was able to do what she had waited so long to do – exhale.

Jamie led her into the restaurant to the table he had for them. Water with lemon had been placed at their seats. He pulled her chair out and waited for her to sit down.

Adriana couldn't allow herself to sit. She excused herself to the restroom. Jamie was perplexed, so he waled to his seat trying to understand her.

Adriana went into the stall and let her tears flow. She put tissue under her eyes to prevent her mascara from streaking down her face. She stayed in the restroom until she could face Jamie.

When she finally reached the table, she kept her eyes low to prevent herself from getting too emotional. Jamie had her chair pulled out and was waiting for her. Then he walked back to his seat and waited for her to speak.

She didn't. When she retrieved her napkin from the table and placed it in her lap, he took that as a sign of her being ready to move on.

"I was shocked when my sister called and told me you wanted to see me," Jamie confessed.

Adriana didn't speak. She lowered her eyes again. Then she looked back up at him.

"I was surprised when Jasmine told me that you had been asking her for years to call me about seeing you. We have never talked about you since our breakup."

"Jasmine told me. I never stopped asking about you," he admitted.

"So, I've learned," Adriana replied. She looked at the menu. She didn't want to reveal that she wanted to know how he was doing and what his life had become.

"Let me see pictures of the kids that could've been mine," Jamie said in a playful tone.

Adriana began to feel a degree of guilt because Jasmine informed her that he had never married and didn't have any children. A part of her wish she hadn't learned that information. She pulled up the photos in her phone; she handed the phone across the table to Jamie. She told him about Ariadne and Nicklous as he scrolled through the pictures. Seeing the longing in his eyes only increased the guilt she felt.

Jamie gently handed the phone back to Adriana. "Do you ever

wonder if we would have had a son or daughter?" Jamie asked as his jaw slightly hardened.

The question took Adriana off guard. She was unaware that he knew about the baby. Jasmine had promised not to tell him until she had the chance to. Telling him about the baby was to be part of the surprise the day she went home early.

"I thought about it the day I called Jasmine."

Jamie picked up the menu and looked at it. Then he looked back at Adriana. "Did you lose the baby because of me?"

Adriana didn't immediately answer his question. She continued to look at her menu. Jamie reached over and lowered her menu.

"Adriana," he began with a cry from his heart. "Was I the reason you lost the baby? I am not asking to bring back bad memories for you." He removed his hand from the menu and placed his five extended fingers to his chest. "I am asking because I need some peace."

Defiance began to arise in Adriana. How dare he ask her for peace? Did he not realize what he had done to them, to her? Reason quickly rose in Adriana to suppress the defiance.

She steeled her eyes then spoke, "It was an abortion. My family felt that under the circumstances, it would be better to have an abortion."

Jamie closed his eyes then dropped his head. "I can deal with that better than knowing my behavior was the reason why our child is not here."

He reached over, touched Adriana's hand then looked her in the eyes, "I can deal with the fact that you did what you had to do."

Those words helped ease the guilt Adriana had been carrying. Adriana lowered her eyes because she could still see the love Jamie had for her. She excused herself to the restroom again.

The waiter was at the table when she returned. They both ordered veal. Moments later, the waiter returned with a Cosmopolitan for her and beer for him. Adriana took a sip of her Cosmo; Jamie looked at her with deep desire as he watched her as he used to. Then he took a sip of his beer.

"My greatest fear was always losing you," Jamie uttered.

Adriana had not prepared herself to hear that. "I've made peace with it throughout the years."

"I had planned for you to be my wife."

Adriana braced herself to walk into the pain. "I was disappointed, too. Gavin is a great guy."

"Jasmine has told me all about him," he said with disappointment.

"Why didn't you ever get married?"

"I never met a woman that I loved as much as I loved you, and I was too afraid that I would hurt someone as much as I hurt you, so I never married."

Adriana didn't have any words for what he just said. She took another sip of her drink. She tried her best to avoid looking in his face.

"I never wanted anyone to grow up without a father like I did, so I chose to get a vasectomy to protect myself and anyone I got involved with."

"Was Professor Hill always married?"

Jamie adjusted his head to look Adriana in her eyes. "What you saw between us didn't mean that Professor Hill didn't love his wife, and it didn't mean that I didn't love you."

"So, I will take that as a 'yes'," Adriana snapped at him.

Jamie understood from the way Adriana responded to his answer that she was still carrying a lot of pain from their relationship.

Again, he placed his hands over hers that were wrapped around the stem of her glass. Jamie cupped her hands inside of his. He looked the love of his life into her eyes. She looked up and saw the pain he was feeling.

"Adriana, men who have sex with men are not necessarily gay; some are bisexual, and some are straight," he told her. "When men have sex outside of their relationships, it doesn't mean they love their girlfriends and wives any less. It's just sex."

Adriana shook her head.

"Women will never understand sex the same way men do," he said.

"No," Adriana corrected him. "Men will never understand sex the way women understand it."

He smiled at her. "You're still doing it. We just said the same thing."

Their conversation was disrupted by the delivery of their salads. Jamie released Adriana's right hand from his left hand to allow the waiter to place their salads on the table. Adriana remembered what it felt like to be loved by him. That feeling frightened her, so she pulled her left hand away.

She picked up her fork and began to eat. Adriana had eaten half of her salad before she resumed their conversation.

"What are you going to do if you meet someone who you really fall for and wants children?"

"I doubt that will ever happen," Jamie said. "I haven't met anyone who I felt like I could get that close to."

"I'm sure you've met some women who wanted to take your relationship to the next level."

"I didn't' say they didn't want to get closer. I said that I didn't feel like I could go to the next level."

"What's keeping you from going to the next level?"

"The woman sitting in front of me."

"I know you haven't spent the last twenty-two years fantasizing about me."

"I don't fantasize about you. I remember the way you made me feel and how I made you feel. I can't forget what it was like when we were together. I haven't met anyone who can make me forget," Jamie explained pointing his right index finger to his right temple.

Adriana was reluctant to believe what he was saying. She was confident the truth was he was more homosexual than bisexual, but she would never say those words to him.

"Well, hopefully if having a wife is what you truly desire, then God is preparing her for you just as he is preparing you for her."

"Vasectomies can be easily reverse. I just didn't want to get trapped into something that I would regret five or ten years down the road," Jamie said as he tapped the table.

He looked over at Adriana's glass. "Are you ready for another one of those?"

Adriana declined the offer because she had to drive home, and her alcohol tolerance was lower than it was when she was in college. They shared updates on their friends from their college days over their entrées.

"You haven't mentioned the girl you roomed with your freshman year. Remember, the one who moved out on you into her boyfriend's room. I will never forget how mad you were," Jamie said with a little chuckle.

"Cilicia," Adriana said.

"Yeah, Cilicia. What ever happened to them?"

"They got married right after graduation."

"Wow! I'm glad to hear their doing good."

"They are headed towards a divorce," Adriana said with sadness in her voice. The thought of Cilicia and Justus reminded her that she had a husband who would be home in less than twenty-four hours. It also reminded her that she was going through something, too.

"What happened?" Jamie inquired.

"Infidelity," was all Adriana said.

"Do they have kids?"

"Yes, two; a girl and a boy."

"It would be nice if they could work it out for the kids at least."

"Not all situations need to be worked out," Adriana said.

Jamie didn't comment on what Adriana said. He didn't want to revisit the last time he saw her, so he changed the conversation.

"What are you doing for the rest of the night?"

"I will probably find something to watch on one of the streaming services," she said with a smile. "Ariadne and Nicklous are at the age where they stay in their rooms if they are not with friends. It's not like it used to be when they were in elementary school. Now, they love to do their own things."

Jamie's heart dropped. Adriana could see the disappointment in his eyes.

"Maybe you will meet the right one and get the chance to experience being a father."

"Love requires understanding, Adriana. I haven't met anyone who I trust enough to find out if she can be understanding."

"You will be surprised at the number of women who are understanding and supportive of their husbands."

"Maybe you're right," Jamie said.

Adriana accepted the offer for dessert. She knew this would be the last time she had dinner with Jamie. Rebuilding herself and her marriage required her to let go of Jamie and any imagination of what life would have been like if she had not arrived at his apartment unannounced. She didn't need to escape to that place whenever she felt disappointment with Gavin. What she and Gavin had was as real as it could get. It is very possible that she could've been in a situation like Cilicia was if she had not witnessed what she saw that day. She could be the one needing a divorce due to domestic violence.

Jamie watched Adriana eat her sundae. He wished he could've shared it with her like they used to share desserts. There was so much about her that he missed. He began to accept that he if ever hoped to marry, he would have to stop measuring people he met by the woman from his past.

They embraced for the last time, and Adriana drove home trying to forget the pulsating sensation Jamie left her with.

25

Because This World Is Mine

Understanding everything she learned in the support group was helping Adriana work through her feelings towards Gavin. She also had to admit that it was helping her understand herself. She used to have fantasies about a woman providing foreplay then her husband coming in to massage the g-spot that caused her to quiver from her sacral chakra down to her feet. No one needed to know about that fantasy because she would never do anything to fulfill it.

Adriana has taken the test. Her results on the Kinsey Scale rated her a one, which didn't really surprise her. Every fantasy she ever had involving women always ended with her ultimately being fulfilled by a man.

Adriana began to recognize that seeing Athra, especially when she walked into the office as opposed to her already being in the office, brought an arousal in her. There was something about the sass in Athra's walk that peaked her sexual curiosity. She couldn't remember feeling this way when they worked together.

As Athra walked to her chair, Adriana realized that it was

something about the way her jumpsuits swayed when she walked that made her the most attractive. She began to understand why men were attracted to a certain kind of woman. Athra was the type of woman whose body movements made her approachable. Was it her confidence or the roundness of her hips? Was it the light in her eyes or the way she pursed her lips? Could it be her walk that commanded respect or her total body?

Whatever IT was, Adriana knew it piqued the interest of both men and women. She was an eyewitness back in the day. She remembered how Athra ignored invitations from men and missed those from women. She shifted in her seat.

As Athra sat across from Adriana, she immediately noticed her face had softened. The lines that were in her forehead were not as profound; her jaw was more relaxed.

"How were your holiday breaks?" Athra inquired.

"Much needed," Adriana admitted.

"That's good to hear."

"I took your advice and revisited by pain with Jamie," Adriana told her.

"Okay; and how did you do that?"

"I met with him over the King Holiday Weekend."

Athra was not expecting that response.

"How did it go?"

"I told him about the abortion I had. He felt relieved because he thought he had caused me to have a miscarriage, so I guess that helped both of us," Adriana exhaled.

"Seeing him and thinking about Cilicia's issues with Justus made me realize that Jamie is probably more homosexual than heterosexual; he has never married and doesn't have children. Our relationship ending might've given him the freedom and excuse to live what is deep inside of him."

Athra was happy to know that Adriana could see the situation that happened between Jamie and her was not a one-off situation. Once a person shows themselves as being abusive, the abuse usually continues.

"What about your relationship with Gavin and the things Cilicia said. We never talked about those things."

A wrinkle formed in Adriana forehead. She lowered her eyes and pursed her lips together. She blinked several times before composing herself enough to answer the question.

She swallowed hard trying to clear the lump in her throat. She fought hard to hold the tears at bay as she looked up at Athra.

"I followed Cilicia's advice to find evidence of what she was saying was true. I checked his gym backpack and found condoms," Adriana admitted aloud to herself and Athra.

She shook her head and took a deep breath as the tears finally flowed out of her eyes. She kept shaking her head.

"I found more condoms in the backpack he carries when he goes to work," Adriana continued as she placed her hand on her collarbone and sobbed.

"I don't know who he used them with, and I'm not sure I want to know. I have been trying my best to understand my own feelings about the whole thing," Adriana confessed, still shaking her head and struggling to speak.

"On the one hand, I am happy that he cares enough about me and my health to protect me by using condoms. On the other hand, he has lied to me repeatedly about being faithful and honoring our vows." Adriana sniffled.

She hugged herself around her waist then began to rock.

Athra sat silently to allow Adriana the opportunity to express what she had kept suppressed for so long.

Adriana sniffled again and shook her head. "I love him, Athra. With every fiber of my being, I love my husband."

She closed her eyes then lifted her head. She exhaled. "I love him, and I want my marriage to work. But I don't know how to allow myself to open my heart to love him like I did this time last year. I want my life back; I want my dream back; I want to know that when I walk inside of a store or the mall that I can do so without wondering if he has slept with any of the people I see.

"I have died, inside of me, again and again since Cilicia showed me the pictures of Blair and Gavin. I've felt like life has left me, and I have just been going through the motions of life for the sake of carrying on. I have sex with Gavin, even when I don't want to; I am afraid if I don't, we will end up like Cilicia and Justus.

"I am trying to find my way back, but he has broken the trust I had in him. If he had been honest with me, then we could have talked about it without me having to be told by someone else.

"I am even too afraid to confront him because I am so scared that it will be over. I am so scared that he will react like Jamie; because if he does, then I will have nothing to hold on to or try to save.

"I'm scared because I want my husband, and I want my family. I feel like I have lost a part of who I am and feel like I will lose even more.

"I am terrified because I feel like if I confront him, I will find out that he is someone I don't know. He might turn out to be someone I don't like. I ask myself all the time who exactly Gavin is in his double life. What does he do in this life?

"It has been hard enough to live with the fact that he is an airline pilot and has layovers in various cities. Hell, a part of me had already accepted that he might have an excursion every now and again during his layovers. But this close to home stuff – my church member who I thought was a friend and the apartment, the swinging.

"God. I have prayed and prayed for answers, but it feels like God is silent. When Gavin is away, I miss him. When he is home, I despise him for what he has done to me, to us. When he is away, I know I don't want to go through life with anyone but him; when he is home, I wish he was still working."

Adriana wiped her face.

"I have decided to not probe any further into whether Gavin has been having sex with men. I already know he has been unfaithful. I don't want to add more pain to my misery because I know I want my marriage to work."

Adriana began to cry again.

"Gavin has never been abusive towards me. He has always been supportive in the things the children and I have wanted to do. Living with him is easy, as my mother has pointed out. He is so loving and caring. He made me believe in all the things I used to dream of as a little girl.

"I just need to find a way to get past this pain that I keep bottled up and really ignored while I was worrying about Cilicia."

Adriana crossed her arms over her chest then titled her head to lay her cheek on her hand. She continued to cry.

"Marriage is the toughest relationship we will ever have. We are expected to work through every challenge that comes our way. It requires us to give up a part of who we are as we become one with someone else. After many years of compromising who we are and denying ourselves, we finally find a way to regain that part we gave up. We only do that when we feel our marriages are secure enough for us to assume a degree of independence while still being interdependent with our spouse."

Adriana looked up at Athra. "Gavin has always been my 85-15 man; his traveling has always made us appreciate the time he was home. I have asked myself if things would be different if he wasn't a pilot."

"What have you decided?"

"If he continues to be the man he is now, then he would still be my 85-15 man." Adriana said, looking off in the distance with a slight smile.

"I think you have made a wise decision, Adriana; no one will ever give us 100% of what we think we want and need, not even ourselves."

Athra paused, waiting for Adriana to continue. Adriana didn't speak.

"Gavin is here, Adriana. He knew you were coming today, and asked if he could join you in this session. I would not allow him to come in here with us unless I had your permission to do so," Athra said.

"What does he want?"

"I think it is best if it comes from him."

"Where is he?"

"I will get him."

Athra returned to the room with Gavin in tow. She sat back in her seat and crossed her legs.

Gavin walked up to the lounge where Adriana was sitting. He got on one knee then placed her hands into his. He looked Adriana in her eyes and could tell she had been crying. He wiped her face with his thumbs.

"I know I've made some mistakes in our marriage that I cannot take back. I'm sorry, Baby," Gavin said.

"You have been a great wife to me and an even better mother to our children. I don't have to worry about things being taken care of while I work. You keep everything in check all the time. I don't want to lose you over my stupid mistakes." He paused, then held her hands again as he lowered his head.

"I've come ask you a question."

"What is it?" Adriana said.

Gavin looked into his wife's eyes. "Will you renew our vows for our 18th wedding anniversary? I want you to know how much I love you and that you are the only woman for me."

Adriana batted her eyes. She paid attention to his words. She looked at Athra then back at Gavin. She thought about her conversations with her uncle and cousin. She even thought about Jamie and the 85-15. She looked at Athra again then at Gavin.

It took her a couple of minutes before she said, "Yes."

"Thank you," Gavin said as he rose from his knees.

He guided Adriana to a standing position then embraced his wife. Adriana allowed herself to melt in his embrace.

* * *

Adriana stepped into her foyer wearing dark blue, skinny jeans, wedged heeled boots, and the royal blue, off-shoulder sweater Catarina had given her for Christmas. She had followed Courtney's advice and used a barrette to pin her hair back on the opposite side of her draping shoulder. Gold hooped earrings finished her look.

Adriana dashed out the door the next time Catarina blew her horn; she was excited and apprehensive. She opened the back passenger side door and slid behind Cilicia. As she was closing the door, she heard Usher singing, "... is your lover?"

"Ooohhh," Adriana said. "I get it. So that's what we're doing tonight?" She laughed

"Only the people in the people in the front are allowed to spark a new flame," Catarina laughed.

The girls' night out was Catarina's idea to help strengthen the sisterhood she and Shanica were joining.

"Going to the 85-15 Group has given me the courage to step outside of my comfort zone," Catarina revealed. "I've spent so much time being the good girl; I want to know what it's like to be a little risqué."

Sheraton and Shanica spent time in cigar bars, so it was not a new adventure for them. However, Adriana and Cilicia had never as much as passed the dutchie on the left- or right-hand side, so it took some convincing for them to agree to go. It was the live music that made Adriana say, "Yes." It was her impending divorce that coaxed Cilicia to go.

Adriana and Cilicia checked themselves and each other when they got out of the car. Adriana pulled up her video chat when they got under good lighting.

"What's up?" the male voice on the other end asked.

"Do you think Cilicia can catch her one?" Adriana laughed.

"Tell her to turn around," Jordan said.

Cilicia did a 360 for Jordan to inspect her groove.

"You better hope you don't see Justus tonight. He might get mad," Jordan joked.

"Thanks for the compliment," Cilicia said.

"And YOU better hope Gavin's not home when you get back," Jordan addressed Adriana. "He's gonna be jealous."

"He'll just have to deal with it," Adriana laughed as she disconnected.

"It's been a long time since I tried to be TLC," Adriana said.

Cilicia touched her hips. "Do you think I could be somebody's motivation?"

"I think we could be somebody's motivation and inspiration as fine as we're looking," Catarina said, rubbing her hands down her hips and thighs.

"You are the baby of the group," Adriana said. "We're sure you'll turn many heads."

Ash & Barrel Cigar Social Lounge was the spot Catarina had chosen. It was recommended by one of her co-workers who had become like a favorite male cousin to her.

They laughed as they walked up to meet Sheraton and Shanica. Adriana was happy to get outside of her mom and wife role. She needed to remember what it felt like to just be; no identity to her husband and children, although they were still in the back of her mind.

Cilicia felt somewhat muddled. Did she really want to have to go back into the shark tank? How would she know if a man would be different than Justus? She slowed her pace to the entrance. She thought about her children and Justus.

She had felt at ease with her decision to proceed through life without Justus; however, looking at the men who were standing on the patio and at the food truck made her think about her days in college before meeting Justus. She took a deep breath.

Catarina looked over her shoulder and noticed that Cilicia was lagging. "Hey, Cilicia; come on, girl. Sheraton and Shanica are waiting for us."

Cilicia took four long strides to catch up to Catarina and Adriana before they entered the lounge. They checked in then listened to the tobacconist talk about the various cigars that were popular among women.

"Do you smoke cigars?" Adriana asked Catarina.

"I have at parties and weddings; it is not something I just do when I'm at home."

Adriana and Cilicia chose a mild cigar with a nutty taste. Catarina decided on a nutty taste, too. The tobacconist opened the door to the lounge.

Adriana felt relieved the moment she walked into the lounge and heard the band playing. Cilicia spotted Sheraton and Shanica, who had found them a spot. It was perfect for the five of them – a couch and five chairs.

Adriana wasn't in her seat for long before she began to sway with the trombonist's solo. She closed her eyes then danced in her seat as the keyboardist joined singing, "Love you, love you, love you."

Adriana was taken out of her trance by the waitress taking drink orders. She ordered her go-to liqueur with a splash of orange juice from her twenties – Grand Marnier. She thought the taste of orange and cognac would go well with the nuts in her cigar. She wanted to remember a time when life was not as complex.

Adriana looked over at Cilicia and Catarina as they sat on the couch and talked about their lives. She looked over at Sheraton and Shanica as they sat beside each other in a pair of chairs having their own conversation. She began to feel like a fifth wheel.

She focused her attention on the band. Seated in a chair near to the trombonist was a man who was sitting alone wearing sunglasses. "I wonder what he's hiding?" she thought to herself.

She looked over to her left again where Sheraton and Shanica were in deep conversation. She could tell by Sheraton's facial expression that something was bothering her. Adriana imagined it had something to do with Shanica's flirtation. Every time she had been around them, Shanica was flirtatious with Cilicia. She looked over at Cilicia and Catarina who had relaxed on the couch and were leaning in to speak to and hear each other. She was happy to see that Cilicia was forming a bond with Catarina. A part of her felt like she was losing something; however, she was happy to know that Cilicia would have someone to help her go through her divorce.

She looked at the band again. The guy in the red puffer vest was still alone. She looked at him wondering what he was all about. Was he a Kappa? What kind of work did he do? Was he here to meet someone? He was sitting comfortably when they got there, so she assumed he had been there a while. Who could be the person he was waiting for?

During the band's intermission, Janet Jackson's *Velvet Rope* came across the speakers. Adriana looked over at the puffer vest man. As she listened to Janet sing, her thoughts took her back to her college days. She allowed her mind to do what it used to do best.

> *He was no longer wearing the red puffer jacket; he was wearing a black leather G-string, and she was in a black, bikini, feline costume holding a burgundy velvet rope. She moved to the beat of the song as she straddled his body. She leaned in and licked each earlobe as she tied his wrists to the bedposts. Then she slid down and licked him in the center of his breastbone. "Who's your cat?" she asked him.*

Shanica walked up behind her and whispered in her ear, "Let me in on the dream," as she returned to her seat next to Sheraton.

Shanica has startled Adriana. She turned her back to red, puffer vest and focused her attention on Sheraton and Shanica.

"What were you thinking about?" Shanica asked as she reached for her cigar. She took a puff then blew a ring.

"Nothing," Adriana answered.

Shanica licked her lips. "I'll believe that if you want me to."

"Maybe she was thinking about nothing," Sheraton said in defense of Adriana.

"Not with that look on her face," Shanica said.

A guy who had been sitting at the bar came over and sat in the chair close to Adriana. He placed his brandy snifter on the table and rested his cigar in the ashtray. He leaned back in the seat then crossed his legs.

Adriana looked over at Cilicia and Catarina.

"Are you ladies having a good time," he leaned into the sofa and asked right before the band began its next set.

Everyone responded with a nod of their heads.

Their conversations continued with the usual questions and answers. Adriana finally walked out to the patio to get fresh air; she didn't want to send a message that would cause confusion in her life. She was enjoying her freedom.

* * *

Cilicia enjoyed being able to sit in an atmosphere where she didn't have to think about anything or anybody else. She was happy Catarina suggested Ash & Barrel because she had never been to a place like that. Even the guy who joined them was a different type of person than what she had experienced in college.

"It's the same game, just more advanced players," Shanica had told them on the way to their cars.

Cilicia was about to fall asleep when her phone alerted her to a text message. She picked up her phone then realized all the messages she had missed from Justus. They were a mixture of accusations, pleas, and threats. She let the aromas from the cigar lounge that lingered in her hair take her mind away from him and return to the peace she felt in the lounge.

26

From This Day Forward

It was Sunday and the day of the Spring Equinox. Regenia and Athra sat in the morning room as they enjoyed a cup of Joe. A lot had changed in eighteen years. Grandma Ethel, Grandma Gina, and Marvin had transitioned from the Earth plane, and Athra had remarried and become a minister. Regenia had spent the past year praying, assisting, and believing in her daughter and son-in-law's ability to work through the challenges they had faced over the past year.

Athra looked out the window at the mourning dove perched on a branch in the backyard. "Marriage is one of the most challenging relationships we will ever have," she said to Regenia.

"I prayed for my children and their future spouses when I separated from their father," Regenia said. "I didn't want them to go through the things their father and I went through."

Athra looked over at her companion. "I do the same thing for my daughter. Divorce brings peace; however, there is still a void that is never filled."

"Divorce is something that is necessary, as we both know. You are right, there is still some sort of void that exists when children are involved because there is a feeling of them being torn apart. I felt that when my parents separated. I know my children felt it when I left their father. Somehow, Marvin's death brought closure to that," Regenia said looking over at Athra, "at least for me it did."

"It is the children that makes me feel this way because I feel as if they are split and torn. I do believe they would've been more broken had I stayed with their father."

"I am happy that Adriana and Gavin have worked things out for themselves and their children. They are both great people and are good together as a couple and as parents," Regenia said. "I was so worried at one point. I stayed on my knees."

"I agree; they are great together." Athra rose from her seat. "I have another stop to make. Thanks so much for the coffee."

Regenia escorted Athra to the door. "Thanks so much for helping my daughter. I will see you soon," Regenia said. She stood and watched Athra leave the driveway.

Adriana, who had gone upstairs after her morning meeting with Athra, returned downstairs and met her mother in the kitchen. "Is Athra's gone?" she asked.

"She has another stop to make. What do you have left to do today?"

"Nothing much. Courtney and Mona are coming to do our hair and make-up at noon. Cilicia and Sheraton are coming for brunch around 11."

"What time do I need to be ready?"

"Courtney is taking care of you today; I think she said between 4:30 and 5:00."

"I just wanted to make sure I don't hold anybody up."

* * *

Cilicia was awaiting the ring of her doorbell. Today was one of those days that brought her happiness for Adriana and Gavin but sadness for herself. She knew she would have to share a space with Justus that would bring back memories of a time when she was mostly happy. She also knew that some part of her would mourn the decision she had made to end her marriage.

This day felt eerily akin to how she felt two months ago when she had to bury her father – it was something she did not want to do but had to do to go forward in her life. She was happy Athra could accommodate her today; she needed the support.

Cilicia opened her door and welcomed Athra into her home. She led her past the kitchen, where Catarina was having breakfast, and into the family room. Cilicia didn't mind Catarina hearing their conversation because she had been sharing some of her concerns with her new tenant.

Catarina had moved in with Cilicia the day after Valentine's Day. The home she shared with her husband had been sold. Catarina's job was going through a merger. She was uncertain what her position in the company would be, so she didn't want to make any long-term decisions until the merger was complete. As a result of both of their transitions, Cilicia offered Catarina the downstairs guest room and Justus's office in the meantime.

Cilicia reclined in her favorite spot while Athra sat in the armchair. Cilicia described to Athra the disquietedness in her spirit. Tears flowed from her eyes as she talked through her thoughts and emotions. Athra sat patiently after Cilicia stopped talking to allow her to settle herself before she began to speak.

"When we truly love someone," Athra began, "the love never dies; it simply transforms into love in another way. To help you understand what I mean by that, I am going to share my feelings towards my ex-husband during my divorce and transition phase.

"It began as love mixed with anger and disappointment. As I

began to analyze our relationship before, during, and after the marriage, I realized the evolution of my feelings. We began our relationship like a lot of young couples, full of love and sexual energy. We married because of that love and sexual energy, AND because we wanted to be good Christians. We thought we were ready. Throughout our marriage, we began to understand things about ourselves and each other that were either suppressed or were not aware were a part of us; it was some of those things that began to drive us away from each other.

"In order for us to have been able to work through those issues, we needed to do individual work and collective work simultaneously, which is challenging to do. The issues that needed addressing were not things we could ignore in ourselves or each other; these are things that led to our divorce because they could not be swept under the rug or ignored.

"My ex-husband and I are among the less than handful of people in our friend group to get a divorce; most of our friends and associates have been able to work through their marital problems. There are times when I come in contact with our friends who have been able to chart through the waters and wonder if we could've made it to their milestones. Every answer is the same for me, 'No; I couldn't have made it in the condition of that marriage.'

Athra paused. Cilicia cried a little more, then looked off into the distance.

"Today won't be easy for me," Cilicia said.

"Yes; today won't be easy for anyone, including Adriana, Gavin, Justus, and the children. However, it is a necessary step in your healing process. The what ifs will cross your mind; that is natural. Allow yourself to feel them but know that God already had a plan for your healing before you began this journey.

"Today you may feel like healing will not come; you may even doubt it a year from now; however, everyone who has experienced what you are going through and growing through will tell you the same thing – there is peace on the other side of this."

"What I don't understand is how he could change so much," Cilicia said through her tears.

"I asked the same question before I left my ex-husband and during the early days of my divorce. Then one day, God led me to a series entitled *Conversations With God*; it was there I found my answer. To sum it all up, God basically says to the writer that people never change who they truly are; they simply grow wiry of pretending who they are not then eventually reverts to who they innately are. Reading those pages brought me more clarity and understanding than I could've ever hoped for. It was then that I began to feel compassion for people who try to be something they are not to maintain a public image or to please people they love.

"Imagine living in a prison that you can never break free of. I do believe that is one major reason why people choose abuse to express themselves; society is ready to deal with symptom treatment but not causes of the effects we deal with in our marriages and other aspects of our lives."

"I want to be so angry at Justus but something inside me keeps telling me to be compassionate in my thoughts and emotions. I still love him; however, setting him free is the best thing I can do for him and our children," Cilicia said as she dried her tears.

"I love him, and I always will."

"Love is like energy. It never dies, it simply transforms," Athra said as she rose to leave.

* * *

It was 6:50 pm when Adriana and Jordan stood at the bottom of the staircase leading up to the mezzanine of the Harvey B. Gantt Center for African-American Art & Culture. The royal blue, floor length gown's bodice and skirt had gold and silver Kundan embroidery and made Adriana look like a princess. She chose the wedding dress because she wanted to embrace her transformation. She carried a cascading bouquet of purple and white orchids.

As soon as they heard Major say, "I found..." they began to ascend the stairs. Gavin had chosen the song he wanted for his wife to make her majestic ascent.

"I don't need to say much to you," Jordan whispered to his younger sister, "because you know Gavin is a great guy."

Adriana smiled as thoughts of her ascending the stairs at the Mint Museum almost eighteen years ago with her father flooded her mind.

"You still have time to turn around if Gavin is not the man you want him to be," Marvin had said to her.

"I love him, Daddy, and I know he will be a great husband and father," was her answer.

Adriana knew the same was still true. She smiled at Nicklous when she reached the mezzanine. Jordan gave his nephew a fist bump as he released his sister to her son to finish the job they shared.

Nicklous checked his watch to see how far off the 6:57 queue of Alicia Keys's "That's How Strong My Love Is" was for him to begin escorting his mother. The song was Adriana's announcement to Gavin of her willingness to work through any obstacles to get to their happily ever after.

Adriana looked past her guests and locked her eyes on Gavin, who was wearing a royal blue tuxedo with a gold vest. His bowtie was royal blue with a gold paisley pattern. Nicklous looked at his mother and smiled. They began their procession during the second verse of the song.

Gavin took a step forward to get a clear view of his wife and son. He felt pride in his son who was wearing a royal blue tuxedo with a cranberry vest and bowtie with gold embroidery. He looked over at Ariadne, who was wearing a cranberry colored, floor length, trumpet dress with gold embroidery.

Seven o'clock sharp was when Athra gave the opening to the ceremony. She asked who gave the couple to be recommitted to their union. Ariadne and Nicklous announced in unison that they did. Then they walked to their spots away from where their parents were standing.

Gavin and Adriana waited as Athra continued her opening. Then she announced. "The seven candles you see here are in the colors of each chakra. Gavin and Adriana will begin their vows," then she walked to the window where a three-tiered candelabra stood.

Gavin led Adriana in taking a step so that the red candle was between them.

Gavin began, "Adriana, my wife. Our love has become firm by your taking the first step when you began walking one with me. Together we shall continue to share all responsibilities of the home, food, and our children that God has blessed us with."

Adriana replied, "Gavin, this is my reaffirmed commitment to you, my husband. Together we will share the responsibilities of the home food, and our children. I promise that I shall do whatever is necessary for the welfare of our family."

Gavin led Adriana in taking another step so that the orange candle was between them.

Gavin: Adriana, my beloved wife, now you have walked with me in the second step. May the Creator bless you. I shall love you and you alone as my wife. I pledge and commit to fill your heart with strength and courage. May God protect our union, home, and children.

Adriana: Gavin, my husband, at all times I shall fill your heart with courage and strength. In your happiness I shall rejoice. May God bless you and our honorable home.

Gavin and Adriana took the third step; the yellow candle was between them.

Gavin: Adriana, now since you have walked three steps with me, our wealth and prosperity will grow. I shall love you with single-minded devotion as my wife. May God continue to bless us; may our children continue their learning and growth. May they be guided by God to live and have long, prosperous lives.

Adriana: Gavin, my husband. I love you with single-minded devotion. My faithfulness to you is pure and you are my joy. May God continue to bless us and our children as we grow in wealth and prosperity.

The couple took their fourth step where the green candle stood between them.

Gavin: My cherished wife, Adriana; it is a great blessing that you have now walked four steps with me. May God continue to bless you. You have brought favor and sacredness into my life.

Adriana: My cherished husband, Gavin; in all acts of righteousness, in material prosperity, in every form of enjoyment, and in the worship and charity of our spirituality, I shall continue to be your partner and greatest supporter.

The fifth step brought the couple to the blue candle that represented communication.

Gavin: My jewel, my wife; now that you have walked five steps with me, my God bless us and make us prosperous in fulfilling the vision we have for our family. I pledge to share in all of your joys and sorrows and to work to bring you happiness.

Adriana: Gavin, my strength; I commit myself to building with you a prosperous family, sharing your joys and sorrows, and to work to bring you happiness.

The lavender candle stood between the couple after they took their sixth step.

Gavin: Adriana, my precious wife; you have filled my heart with happiness by taking the sixth step with me. May wisdom be our guide as we shall fill our home with peace and great joy. May God continue to bless you and our children.

Adriana: Gavin, my darling husband; may God find favor in us and fill our home with peace and joy. I promise to always be with you.

A white candle awaited them when they took their seventh step.

Gavin: Adriana, my crowning jewel, as you have walked the seven steps with me, our love and friendship have become inseparable and firm. We have experienced a spiritual union with God, who is the head of my life. Now you have become completely mine, and I completely yours. May our marriage last forever.

Adriana: Gavin, the most precious jewel in my crown, by the law of God, who is head of my life, and the spirits of our honorable ancestors, I have become your wife. Whatever promises I have given to you, I have spoken them with a pure heart. All the spirits of our ancestors and those who are present here with us are witnesses to this fact. I shall love you forever.

The couple spoke in unison: We have taken the Seven Steps. You have become mine forever. Yes, we have become partners in life and for life. Hereafter, I cannot live without you. Do not live without me. Let us share and celebrate all joys. We are word and meaning, united. You are thought and I am sound. May the morning and night be honey-sweet for us. As Heaven and Earth are stable, so may our union be permanently settled in God's mind.

Athra moved closer to the window and began to speak as Gavin and Adriana circled the candelabra. "Just as God has chosen seven as a sign of completion, so have Gavin and Adriana taken the seven steps in reaffirming their union as husband and wife. The bond Adriana and Gavin have developed is one that shall never be divided because they have sealed their dedication to each other with seven vows before us and God."

Once the couple completed their seventh circle around the candelabra, Athra began to speak again.

"As the Unity Candle is lit, let it symbolize God's eternal love that has been and shall continue to be the beacon of light and wisdom that guides Adriana and Gavin as long as they both shall live."

Athra held up the original wedding bands. "These weddings bands are formed in a circle, which has no beginning and end. Gavin and Adriana will again place this symbol of their commitment to each other and the life they have chosen to live."

After replacing their rings and Athra's prayer, Adriana and Gavin turned to face their family and friends. They proceeded down the staircase to the grand lobby to Whitney Houston and Mariah Carey's *When You Believe*.

* * *

The grand lobby was richly decorated in royal blue and purple with hints of gold, silver, and white. White roses, purple orchids, and blue hydrangeas centerpieces adorned each table.

Spinach balls, mini salmon cakes, stuffed mushrooms, and fried mac and cheese bits awaited the guests as they were escorted to their tables. Attendees were instructed to post all pictures with #gavin&adrianamatthews4ever.

The second course was a curry bisque followed by a Mediterranean spinach salad with Greek dressing. Guests were allowed to take photographs in front of the backdrop that had the seven candles and "Matthews4Ever" written in royal blue and gold.

After cleaning their palates with a mango, lemon sorbet, guests were served their entrée of prime rib with Hasselback potatoes, Macanese grilled chicken over Morrish rice, lamb chops over garlic mashed potatoes, or warm lobster, avocado salad. Asparagus, roasted beet and carrot medley were side dishes.

Family and friends shared their favorite memories of Adriana and Gavin and gave them advice on how to keep the magic alive in their marriage. Jordan toasted the couple. Ariadne and Nicklous gave a toast, too.

The traditional wedding cake was forgone for red velvet and chocolate ganache cakes and bananas foster.

* * *

The wedding directress moved everyone to the rooftop. Gavin had picked Sky High by John Legend for their first dance. He pulled Adriana into his chest; he wanted her to never doubt his love for her. He wanted her to know she had nothing to worry about if breath was in his body. He planted a kiss on her forehead just before spinning her out of his arms to take a bow.

Then, the party jumped off with Mary J. Blige's *Just Fine*. Everyone took to the dance floor as soon as they heard the second beat. Adriana made her way to Cilicia and Catarina then pulled them onto the floor to dance with her. She motioned for Ariadne, Alexus, Nicklous, and Evian to join them, but they shook their heads, "No."

Adriana spun around and saw Winston and Sheraton on the dance floor. She waved; they waved back and gave her thumps ups. She spun around checking out her guests; everyone seemed to be having fun. She grabbed Cilicia and Catarina's hands then lifted them in the air. She sang, "...fine, fine, fine...."

The DJ followed Mary J. with "Set It Off"; Adriana did not leave the dance floor. Cilicia and Catarina stayed with her, then Sheraton, Courtney, and Mona joined them. They joked and laughed about their days before marriage and motherhood. Shanica came in and joined a little later.

Meanwhile, Gavin and Justus had made their way out to the

terrace. They looked towards the Panthers stadium. Justus congratulated his best friend on being able to work things out in his marriage.

"Man, I wish you and Cilicia could work things out," Gavin said to him.

"It's much easier for you," Justus said as he rested his elbows on the rail, looking down on the street. "I was never the man you are and could never be."

"How's rehab working for you?" Gavin asked.

"One hour at a time for me. I've had a few slips, especially when I think about my family."

"My dad used to be a sponsor. Do you have one?"

"Yeah, I have one, but I don't always call him." Justus turned and faced the building. "Going through the divorce should help."

Gavin looked at him with his hands in his pants pockets.

"Don't look at me like that, man. It's hard living this way. I tried to be the man Cilicia needed me to be, but I couldn't do it." He jingled his left hand in his pocket. "I'm tired of walking on eggshells. Living at the apartment, I can relax a little now. I can breathe!"

Gavin motioned to the door to let Justus know they would not be alone. Winston joined them on the terrace. He dapped Gavin and Justus up.

"Your girl's really enjoying herself," Winston said to Gavin motioning his head towards the door.

Gavin gave a little laugh. "She's always enjoyed dancing. She used to stay on the dance floor all night long when we went out. Maybe I need to carry her out more often."

"I hear that," Winston said. "What's up with you?" he asked Justus.

"What's up?" Justus greeted him back.

Gavin dismissed himself to return to the party. "You" by Lloyd was playing when he got back inside. He pulled Adriana, who was drinking their signature cocktail, onto the dance floor. They had to search for a spot on the crowded floor.

When the song was over, Gavin directed Adriana back to the bar to get another of their signature drinks. He stood back and admired the woman who stole his heart.

He never thought about making Adriana the focus of his rekindled hobby. He began to imagine what it would feel like to have his own exhibit in the museum. "The Most Beautiful Woman" could showcase Adriana's transformation from a caterpillar to a butterfly.

Gavin walked over to the photographer and borrowed his camera. He looked through the lens and captured Adriana's movements one frame at a time. She was more beautiful than he realized.

* * *

Jordan surprised Adriana and Gavin with a horse driven carriage to transport them to their hotel suite. Adriana was delighted to have a late night drive up Tryon Street.

She leaned over to Gavin and said, "Do you remember that place?" as they passed the Mint Museum.

He looked at her and said, "How could I forget."

She leaned closer into him for a little extra warmth. The climate had changed in eighteen years and so had the landscape. Adriana sat quietly and enjoyed being in the city she loved so much.

When they reached their hotel room, she was first to shower. She texted Courtney and Mona to style the room while Gavin took his shower.

Gavin stood motionless when he walked into the bedroom. Adriana's body was decorated with pineapple, strawberries, and grapes drizzled with chocolate and caramel syrups. He began eating from his favorite place – her breasts. Gavin savored his midnight snack and shared some with Adriana along the way. Adriana began to giggle when he worked to consume every bit of the syrup from her navel.

When Gavin had eaten her heart out, she pushed him onto his back and straddled him. She let go of the inhibitions that would not allow her to sexually express herself the way she would dream of when Gavin was away. Gavin surrendered himself to his wife. They celebrated their eighteenth anniversary going to the moon.

Adriana slid her body tightly into Gavin. He smoothed her hair back then wrapped his arms around her. Adriana fell asleep knowing that God had answered her prayers. Not only was Gavin with her, so was God.

* * *

Cilicia found the place she could go to escape the troubles of her divorce – cigar lounges. She and Catarina visited as many lounges as they could in the Carolinas. The live music and aroma from the cigars were just what she needed to replace the fog of her marriage and pain of her divorce. Having conversations with some of the men in the lounges gave her the confidence she would need when she decided to date again. In the meanwhile, her relationship with Catarina was what they both needed during their transition time.

The five-spoke wheel was growing stronger, and the rainbow became more vibrant. Cilicia mentally assigned every important woman in her life a color. Shanica – red, Sheraton - orange, Regenia – yellow, Catarina – Green, Adriana – Blue, Athra – white. Violet was saved for her. The awareness she gained from the 85-15 Support Group and Athra's guidance would be needed if she ever planned to marry and love again.

Important Information

The Chakra System

Chakra System and Their Locations in the Body

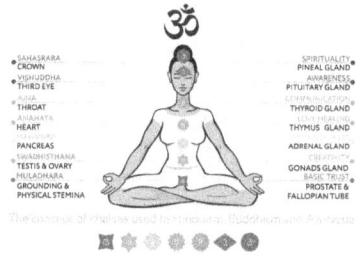

Chakra Meanings and Elevations

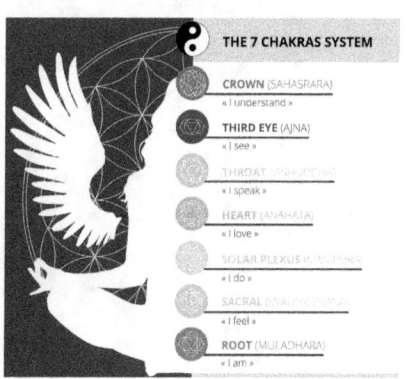

Notes

Tempesta – in Roman mythology, she was the goddess of storms and sudden weather; she could summon powerful winds and wild lightning bolts.

September: Awareness Month – National Suicide Prevention Month, National Alcohol and Drug Addiction Recovery Month, and Health Awareness Month

"Lady Lazarus" - this poem was written by Sylvia Plath who had attempted suicide twice before the age of thirty. It reflects her feelings and approaches to the challenges she was facing in her life, including her relationship with the men in her life, and womanhood itself.

Sylvia Plath – Sylvia Plath authored "Lady Lazarus" and lived with mental health issues. She eventually experienced death by suicide in her third attempt in 1963. Her son experienced death by suicide in 2009.

For Colored Girls Who Have Considered Suicide/The Rainbow is Enuf – this theatrical piece is authored by Ntozake Shange. The author of this book recalled conversations her mother, aunts, and grandmothers had during her childhood about the importance of this work helping women deal with their romantic relationships and the disappointments they faced in life. This work was the inspiration for the 85-15 Support Group because people have many options as to how they will live within the complex of their romantic relationships.

Chakra System – the seven main energy fields located along the spinal cord. They were identified in India over three thousand years ago. The ancient Egyptians believed in over three hundred sixty energy points over the human body. Ayurvedic medicine and people in the far east recognize the importance of having balanced and healthy chakras for good physical and emotional health. They are also important in the spiritual lives of people as recognized by metaphysics. (See picture inserts of the chakra system for more clarity and understanding.)

A Course in Miracles – spiritual, self-study book that has an accompanying workbook whose teachings are designed to help people heal by accepting God and the oneness of humankind.

"Leviticus" – this is a book in the Old Testament of the *Holy Bible*; it contains laws that Moses wrote to instruct the Hebrew people on how to live.

"Matthew" – this is a book in the New Testament of the *Holy Bible*; it describes Jesus's life from birth to death.

Medusa – in Greek mythology, she was human female whose hair was made of snakes and any man who looked upon her face would turn into stone.

Conversations with God – this is a trilogy written by Neale Donald Walsh depicting conversations he had with God that have help bring peace to the lives of people who struggle in different aspects of their lives.

Spring Equinox – is the first day of Spring is generally happens between March 19 and 22; it is the time when the sun beams directly over the equator and there is equal time between day and night. It is connected to renewal and rebirth and was the time ancient people celebrated the resurrection of their gods. It was also a time of cleansing of the souls and homes to generate new energy.

Kundan embroidery – traditionally found in formal attire, such as Indian wedding gowns

Seven – the number seven is a prime number and is associated with the journey towards spiritual awakening and divine guidance. In Christianity, God rested on the seventh day, which symbolizes perfection and completion; cycles begin again after seven years.

Book Club Questions

1. What dilemmas is Adriana experiencing?

2. What are some themes being played out in the book?

3. Do you agree with Athra's interpretation of the *Holy Bible*?

4. Do you think some people get married not being fully aware of their own sexuality?

5. In what ways does the 85-15 Support Group help women deal with the challenges in their marriages?

6. Gavin shows up at Adriana's session in "Because This World is Mine". What message is the author trying to convey to men?

7. Do you think the message the 85-15 Support Group sends to women is the appropriate message for women whose husband is having sex with men?

Resources

Substance abuse, mental health, intimate relationships, and human sexuality are important topics in our society. The following web addresses are resources with vital information to help anyone in need of support or guidance.

The Enlightened Living Ministries – The ELM: https://www.theelm.org

Celebrate Recovery – Christian Based Recovery Group: https://www.celebraterecovery.com

Help for Family Members and Friends of Individuals Impacted by Alcohol Abuse: https://al-anon.org

Help for Family Members and Friends of Individuals Struggling with Narcotic Addictions: https://www.nar-anon.org

The Basics of HIV Prevention: https://hivinfo.nih.gov/understanding-hiv/fact-sheets/basics-hiv-prevention

HIV and Specific Populations - HIV and Gay and Bisexual Men: https://hivinfo.nih.gov/understanding-hiv/fact-sheets/hiv-and-gay-and-bisexual-men

HIV and Specific Populations: -HIV and Women: https://hivinfo.nih.gov/understanding-hiv/fact-sheets/hiv-and-women

Information on the National HIV/AIDS Strategy: HIV and AIDS Resources | HIV.gov

National Alliance on Mental Illness: https://nami.org/Home

National Domestic Violence Hotline: https://www.thehotline.org

National Institute of Mental Health: https://www.nimh.nih.gov/

Suicide Prevention: https://www.nimh.nih.gov/health/topics/suicide-prevention

https://afsp.org

Substance Abuse and Mental Health Services Administration: https://www.samhsa.gov/

Athra Bodhi is an enlightened minister whose purpose in life is to help people have an elevated relationship with God and a better understanding of themselves. She has spent decades on her spiritual growth through her self-study of some of the world's major religions.

www.ingramcontent.com/pod-product-compliance
Lightning Source LLC
Chambersburg PA
CBHW070537010526
44118CB00012B/1152